MW00940203

SANTIAGO, CANTERBURY, ROME

Lessons from the Trails

[handwritten inscription: Steve — I enjoyed swapping stories with you! Steve Cooper]

STEVE COOPER

Other books by STEVE COOPER

SIX MONTHS WALKING THE WILDS
(Of Western Europe);
The Long Road to Santiago

ISBN 13—978-1517795658
ISBN 10—1517795656

© Copyright 2016, STEVE COOPER.
All Rights Reserved.

ACKNOWLEDGEMENTS

My gratitude goes to NorthWest Arkansas Community College, its faculty, staff, and administration for their continued support of the sabbatical program. I hope that this work will in some way validate their confidence in the returns from that investment.

SC

THE GIFT

They didn't exactly walk into my office one day and hand me the gift that changed my life, but it was close to that. The news came via email, and it felt like I had won the lottery.

You know the feeling, right? I can't be the only one that drives down the highway, sees the billboard with this week's lottery totals, and dreams of what I would do first with that amount of money. Not real expectations that it's ever really going to happen, of course, but fun fantasies--cars, boats, bigger boats, extravagant gifts, getting to play Santa for friends and family and strangers, travel beyond the normal vacation route...Sure, I know that's never going to happen, but it's still fun to dream about the changes it would bring to my life.

Never going to happen... but then it did. Not the lottery, exactly, not a bucket of cash. Something better-- the gift of time. What the news brought me was six months of time, a sabbatical from my job as professor of the arts at a community college. My salary would still be paid, so I wouldn't starve, and I had saved so that if I were frugal, I could manage to get to wherever I wanted to go. And maybe even back home again.

Try that fantasy on for size. Swap out the lottery for six months of leave from "real life", and think about where you would go and what you would do. A different climate, maybe? What air would you breathe? Would you need a heavier coat and a fur hat? Snowshoes? Flip-flops and board shorts? A spelunker's helmet with a caving light? A parachute in case your hot-air balloon didn't make it all the way around the world? What food would you taste, what new wine would you sip?

Those questions weren't left for me to answer after the news came. The answers were the reason I was given the chance to spend the time. My plan was already made and if not set in stone, was sketched on maps and manuscript paper.

The project I had proposed was one of the reasons I was awarded the sabbatical. As with most colleges, the program is competitive, and funds are limited. Senior faculty--I crossed into that crew quite awhile back--can apply for a grant of time to further their education, to work on a project that requires time away from the daily routine or requires distance from home. The idea is that an extended block of time to remember why we started teaching and to rekindle our love for the subject that inspired us long ago will translate into a return to the classroom with renewed energy, a fresh perspective to offer students.

The United States is one of the industrialized modern countries that doesn't really believe in the power of this concept. Generally, only universities and religious institutions offer the awards, and only in very limited numbers.

In other advanced nations, sabbaticals are recognized for the value they bring to the workplace as well as to individuals who experience them.

A sampling:

At the beginning of this century, Sweden began experimenting with a program that allowed workers to take up to a year for pleasure or study or skill training, with their work positions being filled by unemployed people.

Eurofound is an EEU foundation that works to improve living conditions in the European Union. (www.eurofound.europa.eu)

France allows anyone with certain levels of professional experience and longevity at a company to apply for up to eleven months of sabbatical leave. Though it is generally unpaid leave, the workers retain social service benefits, and the job is protected for their return.

It is fairly common in Germany to have the right to request three-to-twelve month sabbaticals with some level of pay and a guarantee of a job upon your return.

Here in the USA, we're still mired in the old way of thinking that preaches work, work, work until the day you retire, then hope that your health is sufficient to allow you to "rest" in your old age. Time away from the job--beyond the typical two weeks per year--has been considered a waste and "too expensive" to allow.

More studies are beginning to convince employers that extended time away from work is beneficial not only to individual workers, but also to the bottom line of the companies that employ them.

Inc.com, a company supporting entrepreneurial projects, reports that nearly a quarter of the Fortune 500's top 100 companies to work for offer some form of sabbaticals.(3) Writing for CNN Money, Jeannie Sahadi says that US businesses who offer their veteran employees paid or unpaid leave find that it helps "...build loyalty, increase retention, and foster greater creativity at work."

Although more US companies are beginning to recognize the value of sabbaticals in retaining their best employees, the feature has traditionally been the province of colleges and universities. One of the reasons I chose the profession I did was the chance to enjoy this feature of the work life--extended sabbatical leave to continue pursuing inspirational study. Our school is a young one and only began awarding a very limited number of sabbatical leave grants during the past ten years.

I had applied in the Fall of 2013 and been told that there were insufficient funds available for a grant, but a slight rise in the school's budget the next year prompted the awarding of one leave. I was given notice of the leave that would begin with the spring term of 2015 and immediately began making plans to rework my proposal for that calendar.

Packing for a long walk is part of the fun. Laying out all the gear and clothes on the guest bed, shopping for a few new little travel toys, printing maps...it all builds the excitement of the trip. I don't worry too much about weight anymore since I've done this enough times to know that I can carry whatever I can fit in the bag. However, there's a finite amount of space in that backpack. There's only so much gear I can stuff in the pack, and it's not good if the thing is filled to bursting every time I need to hunt through it for that one particular item.

I find myself negotiating with the gear, shifting bits from one side of the bed to the other. The left side for the "gotta have it" stuff, the right side for the "if there's extra room" (yeah, like that's gonna happen), and then a side table for the extras. ("Surely this is so small that it will be easy to squeeze in there somewhere!") Usually nothing but the left-side pile makes the final cut, and then some of it gets thrown out when I realize I've forgotten to stuff in my jogging shoes or a third little language guide.

New items--an iPad, and a couple of pounds worth of cables, chargers, adaptors, an extra shirt or two, duplicates--an extra pair of socks and shorts so I won't have to do the wash quite as often, a second hat, and always, always, too many notes and sketches of project ideas.

There's something about getting away from everyday life that turns on the faucet of ideas. Projects and stories and songs pop up out of thin air. Things that didn't seem possible suddenly appear easy. Inspirations that never grew in the past suddenly blossom. Energy arises where in normal life there would be none.

Life grows into routines, if not ruts. Work and order and normalcy dampen creative impulses...or at least provide an excuse for ignoring them, pushing them to a back burner while "necessities" are accomplished. Daily work takes precedence, is given precedence, and the work of the soul recedes into the shadows, waiting for the attention of a few occasional moments. Rather than being the focus of a life, the creative urge slides into position as an afterthought.

This is why I walk...to set the stage for life-changing, pattern-changing effort. An abrupt departure from "real life" jars the consciousness, shakes the spirit.

So, my pack always has a few too many notes from works-in-progress, lyrics I'm trying to massage into songs, story ideas, sketches of scripts that have yet to be written. Most of the time this little piles returns home intact, unfulfilled, a little more rumpled, with an extra coffee ring on one page and another corner soaked from the rain that hit while I was having a nap sitting against the side of a country church. It's OK, though--there must be something about having the work with me that feeds me the beast.

The trail in Spain is so lined with hostels that pilgrims there need little aside from a change of clothes. I'm a little envious of a couple of my friends who are stronger than I am when it comes to loading the pack. They both were scrupulous about weight and were able to walk with packs that totalled 13-14 pounds, pack included. I seem to go the other direction--throw in a little of everything, and then leave a trail of droppings along the way when I get tired of hauling the extra weight.

One morning walking along the Camino in Spain near Zubiri I came across a woman sitting beside the trail, crying softly. She was sitting beside a huge backpack, and was also wearing a large belly pack. I asked if she were hurt. She said she had just come to the point where she couldn't continue with her heavy pack, but she couldn't bear to part with any of the "stuff" she'd loaded for the walk. She was one day into the walk and had hit a wall of weight.

I have my own useless worries, but the pack isn't one of them. Loading the backpack, for me, is more of a game. It's building the excitement of another adventure. It's a bit of pre-departure anticipation of the fun I know I'll experience on the road. None of the junk I carry is worth stressing over, so it's just an exercise in play, like deciding which piece of candy to pick at a candy store. The walking life has returned far more than it's taken, so I anticipate every minute I get to spend on the road.

My plan for this trip was a simple one...in theory anyway. I planned to walk a thousand miles across Europe on the Via Francigena, studying the culture, the history, and the arts along this thousand-year-old pilgrimage. Although I had requested a leave that would allow me to begin during spring weather, I wasn't about to argue when the word came that I could leave in January. I closed my house, turned off the water, garaged the car, loaded my backpack, and headed for London.

THE EASIEST AND THE CHEESIEST

...and a month later found myself slogging through cold, driving January rain on the edge of a two-lane Italian highway, no shoulder, oncoming Fiats and Peugots and Maseratis buzzing me like a swarm of pissed off wasps. Not the romantic vision I'd had of a picturesque walk through a sunny, warm countryside. And yet, it was still more fun at the time than being back in the normal classroom routine.

"Normal classroom routine". There really is one, but anyone who's tried to manage a classroom knows that "normal" is more about the planning than the execution. We deal in agendas, lesson plans, dividing every class period into slices of a time-pie, figuring which bit of content we can squeeze into a 10-minute or 20-minute bite, working out strategies for getting the material from our heads into theirs. Then we step into the classroom where real people exist, and those strategies have to bend to the needs of those realities. The best teachers I know get it--we're there first of all to teach people...the content is just the means to help us lead them to a place with more options.

When we teach our children in public schools, we focus on content. The necessities of meeting common core testing standards--or whatever the flavor-of-the-decade happens to be--narrows our vision down to nuts and bolts, just the basics of the 3 Rs. The good teachers somehow find the time to go beyond that low bar to set a context for the material. Almost all teachers spend some amount of time on citizenship, or deportment, or group behavior...but it's at the level of a survival skill. The teacher's survival. The only way to live through a year--or even a single class period--at the head of a phalanx of hormonal teenagers is to instill in them some notion of the need to live together in peace. It's either that, or use a whip and a chair, and those aren't legal in most states.

I believe most would agree that we generally don't get beyond that level of achievement in social behavior. We rarely climb above that level of the pyramid, leaving our students--unintentionally, of course--with the idea that as long as they learn content, they'll live happily ever after.

We don't teach happiness. We don't teach our students how to live a full life. We don't have a curriculum that helps guide our own children, the children of our neighbors, the kids who will one day be our own neighbors, and teachers, and...gulp...caretakers, what it means to be a self-realized being.

Our eyes are so locked onto the bottom Maslow steps that we're not helping lift our students' eyes to those higher rungs. We're not teaching them how to be happy. If we don't teach them those lessons, they'll study with a different teacher, and too often that is the television or the internet. And of course, we're not talking about PBS or the "good" Internet, filled with all the knowledge of a vast world. We're talking about the easiest and cheesiest of both. They'll find the Jerry Springer, Naked and Afraid, the universe of reality TV and cute-cat videos--the media junk-food that tastes good for a minute, but then leads to clogged mental arteries.

Parents do their best to teach their children to eat well, but all have seen what happens if you turn a kid loose in a candy store--they'll eat themselves sick. They'll gorge on their favorite treats to the point of illness. Until they're old enough to think for themselves, until their brains have developed the actual connections that allow them to control impulses, the adults in their lives have to help them control those wayward appetites. A snack now and then is fun, but a steady diet leads to nothing but lazy, fat asses and thick, slow brains.

If we don't teach them how to be Real People, how to lead Real Lives, they'll go to school with the Kardashians and Paris Hilton.

A WINTER WALK

"The Rain in Spain Stays Mainly in the Plain". The rain in London stays everywhere, wherever it wants to be, all winter long. If the air isn't wet, it's gray, and if it's not gray, it's...well, it's always gray or wet in January in London. And so it was both when I arrived.

The flight from Arkansas to London was uneventful. Long, but uneventful. And still one of the most fun days of my life. Finally getting to start the Via Francigena had me jazzed and ready for anything.

...Even the rain. It's true--if you go to the UK in winter, you expect rain, but it's not the frog-choking downpours we get in the southern US. Mostly it's a pervasive, quiet, soaking, cold drizzle. For a day or two I didn't mind living with it. The idea of walking for a month in it didn't thrill me, however, and I had made alternate plans.

I'd been studying the "French Route" from Canterbury--an hour by train southeast of London--to Rome for several years and thought I had a fairly good handle on what to expect. I'd logged lots of miles during several trips on Spain's more famous El Camino de Santiago, and those walks had led me to look for other outlets for my addiction to walking.

The previous summer I'd walked for a week or two on the beginning of the road from the Canterbury end, moving a couple of hundred miles into France, and a few years back I'd crossed the Alps at the Col de Gran St. Bernard, the highest point on the route leading from

Switzerland south into the Val D'Aosta in Northern Italy. I discovered that there weren't many trekkers on this trail yet. The Spanish trail draws more than 100,000 hikers every hear, mostly between April and October. The Francigena sees only a few hundred during the same months.

The relative quiet of the route as well as the geography made it seem a natural option for a long walk. It was another thousand-year-old cultural trail that would take me through France, Switzerland, and Northern Italy as well as a tiny bit of the UK. What's not to like about that plan?

An Archbishop of Canterbury, Sigeric the Serious, had traveled that long, long way--especially long by Medieval transport, I'd guess--in 990 A.D.,heading to Rome to be invested with the office of Archbishop. On the return trip, he and his scribe listed the 80 stops they made along the way. This simple list became one of the first written "guides" for travelers.

I had done lots of prep work on the actual path I'd walk, but I decided on a whim to try and get a look at that document when I landed in London, before starting the actual walk. I landed mid-day in the rain--Did I mention that London in winter is usually wet???--and slogged mistakenly to the British Museum. (So much for my thoughtful planning.) I realized my error, that I actually needed the British Library, but it was difficult to hurry away from the museum. It's one of my favorite places in a great city.

Soon, though, I sloshed a few blocks northwest to the great library beside the picturesque St. Pancras rail station. They claim to be the largest library in the western world, and it's easy to believe. It was fun to experience the place for the first time with no real preparation. Even though I hadn't done my homework like a good researcher should, the visit was a wonderful way to begin the adventure.

Before I could use the resources of the Manuscripts Room, I had to register as a "reader" with the library. I arrived at the office just as they were going to close for the day. The man at the front desk welcomed me, and rather than brush me off till the next day, as many offices might have done, he turned to a colleague across the room and called, "Roland, we have a visiting scholar who needs to be registered. Could you do his ID before we leave?" Someone shoved a pen and a form in my hand and said, "Just the top three lines, Mate...I'll do the rest," while another said, "Sit here and give us your best American smile for the camera." Just like that, I had a photo ID and directions upstairs to the Medieval Documents.

I followed their directions to Manuscripts, and there, too, I was treated like family. I'd not booked a time nor done an advance request for the document I needed, but instead had hope to make this just a "reconnaissance visit", learning the layout and what I would need to do on my return. The staff, there, however, insisted on trying for a quick grab of the manuscript rather than ask me to make another trip back. They weren't able to gather the folio on short notice, but I did get to have a look at a facsimile on CD that gave me the information I needed.

I left the library feeling like a lucky man. I didn't realize at the time that my new ID would later prove to be a valuable ticket out of trouble.

ST. PANCRAS TO ROME

St. Pancras has no shortage of pubs and cafes, and I retreated from the rain to a cozy Mabel's Tavern off St. Eustace Road to have a Guinness and a think about my options. I'd bought a $50 Ryanair one-way to Rome in case I decided to begin there, and it was decision time. A hot plate of sausage and mash went down well with the beer. Sitting there warm and dry, well-fed and watching the rain wet everyone but me, I was reminded that there was no wrong answer here. I was looking at months of freedom from routine, a long road ahead of me, enough walking to smooth over any old frustrations and distractions. It didn't really matter where I started.

However...I'm a Son of the South and grew up in sunshine. Backpacking is a lot more fun in warm sunshine than cold rain. I was starting this in winter and wanted to aim for the best weather possible. While the thought of ending in St. Peter's Square at the Vatican was appealing, the thought of spending the next 2-3 weeks beginning the walk in cold drizzle...not so much. The next day found me headed out to Stansted Airport early enough for another coffee before the cattle-call flight to Rome. We moo-ed and ahh-ed as we were herded onto the plane, but I don't mind a little herding to save a buck. (For all its lack of luxury, that airline does have a great on-time arrival record.)

We landed at Ciampino, the smaller suburban airport on the south side of Rome, in time for me to have my pack on and moving by mid-afternoon. For most on the Francigena route, the trail begins or ends at St. Peter's, but I'd decided to start my pilgrimage with the first steps off the plane, following the Appia Antica into the heart of the city.

From London's wet cold, I exited Ciampino to a sunny, 50F afternoon. Any doubt that I had made the right choice to start in the south evaporated like the last drizzle on my pack. There couldn't have been a nicer day to wander the half-mile over to the south end of the Appia Antica and start up those old paving stones toward the Eternal City.

I'd overloaded my pack again (of course), but I hardly felt the weight as I hit the road, crossed over the roaring traffic of the SS7, and turned north onto the quiet trail toward Rome.

The sun was low and would be down before I reached the Circo Massimo, but I decided to chance it anyway. It was a beautiful cool afternoon with nothing but blue above. Only a few cars risk their suspensions on the old stones, so I shared the way mostly with a few joggers, a cyclist or two, and a few curious farm dogs. The 13k walk into town should take me only a couple of hours, but I spent another hour stopping to shoot photos along the way. The old Roman Road is now preserved as an archeological park and can be a magical path into the city. The Roman pines, a distant aqueduct, and the bits of walls and statuary that line the straight old road are hard to walk past without stopping to consider the other travelers they've watched pass by. I staggered into the heart of the city after dark, but with no danger other than facing down city drivers on the narrow way. Another hour of staggering led me to my hotel, where I went down hard.

The road was built in the 4th Century to connect Rome to the southeastern port city of Brindisi.

It was designed to allow two chariots to pass side-by-side and must have seemed like a superhighway at the time. These few miles on the south side of the city are now an archeological park, passing by catacombs, aqueducts, arrays of sculptures, and rows of Roman pines. If you walk it in the evening, you might glimpse some of the ghosts of the thousands of slaves who were crucified and hung beside thee road after the Romans quelled the revolt led by Spartacus in 73ad.

I staggered into the heart of the city after dark, but with no danger other than facing down city drivers on the narrow way. Another hour of staggering led me to my hotel, where I went down hard.

Sara at the hotel desk showed me the shortcut through the alley up to a street where I could find dinner. I wanted to explore the neighborhood, but I didn't have it in me. The first little cafeteria I saw called to me. I collapsed into a chair and dug into a plate of vegetable parmesan that was a fine end to my arrival in Rome.

TIME IS A LUXURY

Time was the greatest luxury of this walk. It's the one element none of us are promised in our lives, but teachers lives revolve around the clock. Our bodies are geared to the school-year cycle, and they print special calendars for us. Our days are regimented by class changes, and every hour is broken into problems and projects, group exercises and quizzes, lectures, power-points, conferences with students, parents, administration.

Time off task--or on broader, horizon-stretching tasks--doesn't just appear. A teacher has to plan that into the work, or it just doesn't happen. So many demands are made on teachers' class time that most of us fall into the pattern of concentrating only on the basic core of the curriculum, the essentials that must be covered in order for the students to move on, or to score well on the tests.

But tests measure skills or content knowledge, not a mastery of life. Exams don't tell us if we've trained a student to be the kind of person we would want as a citizen of our town, as a neighbor, as a possible partner for one of our own children.

Somewhere in that time-crowded day, we as teachers must find a a way to drive in a few more teaching wedges, lessons on how to be real people, how to raise students' eyes from the immediacy of content to see a bigger goal down the road. Of course we want to teach the facts and skills that give them a better chance at jobs and careers, but we also must realize that we may be the only factors for fulfillment in the lives of many of these future adults.

As teachers we hold them captive for hours at a time. We have their attention for more time than perhaps anyone else during a normal day. We are parent substitutes for some, and for others the only professionals they meet on a regular basis. We are occasionally role models, whether we ask for that job or not. As we find ourselves in that position, it's incumbent on us to work with our students not only on content, but also in guiding them toward happier, peaceful life paths.

Part of what I'm advocating we teach is a type of work ethic, the need to complete projects, to see an idea through to a logical end. This idea is one we all embrace regardless of our teaching discipline and is thus easier to justify in the crowded schedule. Students must be guided to learn the pleasure of finishing a task if they're to succeed in any field.

They're being counter-trained daily to shorten attention spans, to lose focus, to be distracted by every pop-up "squirrel" that crosses their line of sight. Imagine the hundreds of visual clay pigeons flying past them hourly as they gaze in reverence at phones and tablets, practicing diligently at having less ability to concentrate on longer-term work. This is the trend teachers must buck if they want to build thinking adults who can see far enough down the road in front of them to reach the end.

Occasionally that end might be something other than the original goal, since I'm not talking about blindly following fixed routes. Failures along the way to a target will often alter the direction an exploration will take. We know we have to embrace "learning failures" as a means to illuminate the way to success.

WALKING IN ROME

I'm in Italy again, and yesterday I had my first gelato since landing. I always forget just how good that first taste can be. I know it in my head, I remember it when I'm home, but there's nothing like that sensation of the first tangy bite on your tongue.

The thought reminded me of other "firsts" along the road. I've been fortunate enough to travel this area a lot, but each time the first glimpse of the Mediterranean gives me a little bump.

I saw it this time from the window of a Ryanair jet, and I'd had "another first" reminder that they are first and most importantly a discount airline. Comfort and convenience are not their watchwords. They do everything they can to save a buck short of herding us passengers with cattle prods.

Actually I think that might be coming. This airline made news a couple of years ago by announcing that their in-flight toilets would become the pay kind. They backed off of that plan, but they still manage to make everyone feel like a number more than a real live human being.

An example is that they have countless add-ons to their ridiculously cheap ticket prices, all meant to raise that profit margin just a tad. This time I paid an extra 10 pounds sterling for "priority boarding", just to see if it put me a step ahead of the herd in claiming a seat. (Most are non-reserved, grab-what-you-can.)

I was pleased to have a special "Priority Boarding" line at the gate and arrived in time to be first in line. After a short wait, though, during which the line grew behind me, the announcement was made for a gate change--the gate next to ours. Which meant, of course, that as the mob shuffled next door, I was now at the back of the line. No worries, though, since we were "boarded" down a flight of stairs to be loaded onto buses, priority boarders mixed with the great unwashed non-priorities, and hauled out to the plane for a free-for-all rush to seats.

And yet, even after all that de-humanizing creativity, I still fly them. They're cheap, and they arrive on time. I wish we had them in the U.S. And, each time I'm here again, the hassle is like the first annoyance all over again.

No matter. When I stepped off the plane in Rome, I grabbed my backpack, walked out of the airport, and smelled the warm, humid Italian air for the first time again as well. That pleasure balances lots of travel hassles.

I spoke to a few folks on the way out of the airport, trying to remember my Italian repertoire. A few years previously I had spent a week at a language school in Chiavari, a historic little city on the Ligurian coastline, just southeast of Genoa. The school was another first for me, as my deficient Italian has come from cafes and hotels and other hikes through the country. This means, of course, that I have no real grammar and can survive only with enough hand gestures and desperate charades.

Since I had the time, I'd decided to use the next day to dry out, enjoy the city, gather my wits, see if I could fit them in the backpack while I strolled through Rome. The next day was predicted to be a sunny Wednesday, and I wanted one more day without the weight of the pack before I headed north.

Rome is a great city for wandering. Not only are there welcoming cafes at every turn, but the walkways beside the river open a window to life on that waterway. In the winter the leaves are off the trees and the view is open. The moving water stirs a breeze, and always there are joggers and boaters birds to study. On this trip I wandered through Trastevere on the southwest of the center and then strolled the Tevere up to St. Peter's Square.

It was mid-January, but the Vatican was still cloaked in nativity scenes inside the basilica and out on the square. There are fewer busloads of tourists in the winter, but it looked like all of them were gathered for photos by the manger scene in the plaza. A forest of selfie sticks joined the palm trees in the Roman Bethlehem. The soundtrack to the scene featured church bells and police sirens that are always present in the Rome soundscape.

The Swiss guards in their bright colors kept watch from the doorways, seemingly only decoration, but occasionally jerked from boredom to action by real trouble. It's not been that many years since an intruder attacked Michelangelo's Pieta inside the basilica, damaging the sculpture and necessitating its move behind protective plexiglass.

Now at the entrance there is a metal-detector checkpoint as well as the inspection for proper attire. Some of my students on a performance tour tried to test that one a few years back and were turned away at the entrance for wearing shorts or having bare shoulders. (One of the guys decided to buy the "paper pants" on sale at local souvenir stands; others just bailed and missed the experience.)

I wanted to visit the basilica again before I began walking. It felt like a kind of grounding of the adventure. Plus, I hadn't been inside in several years, and I love the feeling I get when I step inside that amazing structure. Sure, the cynical side of me tries to pull me back with thoughts of the downside(s) of that religion (and all religions), but from strictly an architectural standpoint, the place is awe-inspiring. The fact that several hundred years ago, a group of people conceived of the place, designed it, and brought it to life still moves me.

If I were one of those more directly damaged by actions of church officials, I'm sure my reaction would be different. I missed out on those tortures, though, and can squint past them to see the beauty of this monument. To focus on the ugly side of the history would lead us toward acts like the Taliban--destroying treasures of other cultures through religious zeal.

As I write this, the online news sources are spreading the word of the coming end to another incredibly long building project, the cathedral La Sagrada Familia in Barcelona. Now approximately 130 years into the construction, the managers of that wonder hope to complete the final towers in 2030, soon enough that most of us may be able to see the end to a project begun during our great-grandparents' youth.

The scope of these monuments is stunning to me. I wonder at the clarity of vision and the zeal of those who were able to convince enough wielders of power to begin a plan that could not be finished in a single lifetime. Many of those churches--the Duomo in Florence, for example--were begun without the knowledge of how the most difficult parts could be built. The first steps were taken with the faith that someone would eventually be able to engineer an ending

Stepping into the depths of St. Peter's on that winter day in 2015, though, I wasn't worried about how

I would reach the end of the trail. Mine was an easier walk. The maps were drawn, and many had traveled the way ahead of me. My challenge was just the fun part-- the physical effort of moving through that many miles. My heart was light with six months of freedom to walk waiting for me outside the door, the beginning of what I knew would be an incredible opportunity to move, and breathe, and eat and rest, to drink and think my way through some of Europe's most beautiful ways.

JOURNAL, WEEK 1-2

Wednesday 1/14/15

Who knew? The same cafeteria from last night is on my way toward the Via Trastevere and the city center. I stopped in for a cappuccino and croissant before making my way to the river. It's a mild day in the city, the kind of day that makes you want to just let go of the map and wander. Sooner or later you'll find your way back home, right? Rome is a great city for surprising little bars and cafes tucked away in tiny piazze that aren't marked on the tourist maps. The Cafe Umbria is one I found this morning for a second coffee. The regulars flowed through the place, the most friendly and obviously most popular being Selena, a small schnauzer who stepped in, made the rounds to all 6 tables to greet everyone, then left to continue her morning rounds.

The Campo die Fiori was filled with a morning market and a batch of Selena's cousins out walking their owners. I wandered through the stalls and made my way back to the Tevere, across the river, and toward the Vatican. I was in search of a stamp for my pilgrim's credential, the "passport" that would signify my status as a pellegrino in La Via Francigena.

Since I've decided to walk north from Rome rather than south from England, I'm in effect doing the pilgrimage in reverse. The adage that "All roads lead to Rome" is on the cover of my credential, and most hikers on this route choose to end in Rome at St. Peter's Basilica. That was my plan as well, but getting to start the walk in winter changed that plan. It's an easy rationalization for me, though, since Sigeric's document listing the stops he made on his journey in 990ad was actually written on his return journey to Canterbury. My friend and semi-famous Arkansas historian Professor Kiser has suggested that to be legitimate I need to walk backwards the whole way, but I've decided I'll ignore his advice. Professor Laughton drew up a graphic document proposing a pogo stick, but I'm also ignoring that along with his comments about turnip trucks. For me the goal is not Canterbury or Rome but just to be on the route, being present on the walk for the entire journey regardless of compass points. Or pogo sticks.

The sight of St. Peter's Square in the Vatican is a stirring sight, an architectural monument that always impresses. Today, mid-January, their large manger scene is still featured prominently near the column in the center of the square. The Sacristy is a small chapel on the west corner of the basilica. Giovanni, a security guard on duty, led me across the velvet line and into the room to receive my stampa on my credential, and I was ready to go.

Thursday 1/15/15

Freezing temps and blue skies for my walk into town and out of the city. The Via Cassia runs part of its way beside the river before climbing out of Rome's valley. 20k or so of climbing later, I found the Cassia Hotel in La Storta. Salvtore, at the desk, rented me a room with a smile, and I crashed hard, partly from the climb, and partly from sucking diesel and car fumes beside the road all day.

Friday, 1/16/15

More walking beside a busy highway today. Not nice walking, but putting some miles between me and Rome. Felt the aches and pains of a cold or just being out of shape. When I hit Poggio Dell'Ellera, I took the first place I could find---Il Postiglione. The inn had been a postal stop since 1463 according to their documents. The stone stairways had been worn smooth and then beyond that, with a multi-century dip in the middle of each step. The grounds include a pool, a large formal Italian garden, and a 30-meter section of a Roman road that has been excavated and preserved near the parking lot. Dinner was beside a welcome wood fire. A pianist played valiantly for me and the two other tables of guests. Breakfast the next morning was a bit embarrassing as the hotel put out an entire buffet just for me. I didn't complain. Up the road I know there will be a few meals of nuts and a bite of old chocolate, or a handful of crackers and an olive, or a bowl of powdered soup. I'll take the private buffet when it's offered.

Saturday, 1/17/15

I had decided to walk a shorter day today climbing over a ring of hills surrounding Lago di Bracciano to a the lakeside town of Trevignano Romano. I quickly made it a 4k longer day by trusting a Google map that led straight into a private farmyard guarded by two vicious dogs. (Actually they put up a vicious front but succumbed to ear-scratching like most dogs will. My phone map kept trying to get me to do 5k along a 2-lane highway with tight guardrails and no shoulder. A local farmer pointed me to an alternate country lane straight over the hill which worked great until the rain hit. It was a cold, hard drenching, the first of this hike, so I've now been initiated.

I was also reminded that even walking through a cold rain, the walking life is a good one. Stepping into a warm cafe on a cold day is rarely a bad thing thing, but it's even better after hiking a few miles in a cold rain. Shucking the poncho, shaking the rain out of my hair-- allow me my fantasy, please--and drying off in a warm corner with a cafe latte and a good book may be one of the nicest small pleasures in life.

Trevignano Romano is a quaint little town with a solid perch in the hills on the north bank of the lake. Dalia, my B&B host, is an actress from Sweden by way of Rome, and she keeps a colorful Bohemian apartment with a nice view of the lake.

Sunday 1/18/15

A week on the road. I celebrated early with an extra cappuccino and started climbing the mountain out of town. The nice thing about walking Sundays in the country is that smart people stay home...only hikers and bikers work the roads. My target today was Sutri, a historic Etruscan town just about 8 miles north as the crow flies. (10 if you have to walk.).

Greeting me on the way into town was a wall of tufa stone in an archeological park 1k east of the centro storico. Carved into the side of the wall are rows of empty Etruscan tombs, some the size of a single garage, some closer to a bread box. They date from before the first century. The trail beside the wall leads to a similarly-carved Roman amphitheater, cut into a mountain of tufa. It's a fourth the size of its Rome cousin but impressive still.

Albergo Sutrium is my home tonight. I've already had a shower, a nap, and a great lunch of salad and pappardelle con cinghiale (wild boar). The festival of San Antone is on this week, but I think I've timed my stop to miss most of the excitement. The banners are still out, but the fervor is dying.

Monday, 1/19/15

Sutri to Vetralla--a frosty morning, and I was so taken with the views that I missed a turn, added 2k to my day. Too much walking on the side of Via Cassia today...too much exhaust smoke in the air.

Climbed a steep staircase into Capranica, another hilltop town past Sutri.

Vetralla...found a great ristorante/pizzeria...with no pizza. Had to settle for fried lamb chops and salad. Life is hard, but a man's gotta do...

Tuesday 1/20, 21

A rainy, drippy day. Climbed more hills and dodged drops into Tobias for a break at Bar Amnesia. Nice little woodburning fireplace going, but there was a strange, unfriendly vibe in the air. Got out after a quick coffee. Made it to Viterbo, my first "city" on the route in time for lunch at the Shaker Cafe (as in "shaken, not stirred") in time for lunch before checking in at an Airbnb connection, the Easyroom B&B. Marco and Linda were sweet hosts, and the room had a full bath. Nice treat--a hot bath after a morning walking in cool spitting rain.

Wednesday is a rest day in Viterbo, and I'm ready for one.

Wednesday, 1/21/15—Viterbo
(THERE USED TO BE A ROOF)

The cardinals were stuck--the French camp against the Italian camp. They were trying to elect a pope, but after a year of deliberations (?!), the sides were dug in. Their hosts in Viterbo started to get a little impatient and decided to push the matter. When verbal pressures failed, architectural schemes were laid. The roof came off the meeting house where the cardinals were holding their non-deliberations, and meals were reportedly reduced to bread and water. The redhats were locked in to their conclave ("con chiave") until a decision was made.

It's a famous tale here in the walled city of Viterbo

I'm remembering a time in Spain when I had just returned to walk a long trail again after having done it the year before. After a day or two on the same trail, feeling the muscle aches and stiffness, the weight of my overloaded backpack, listening to the snores--or worse, the cell-phone chatter--of other hikers in the hostels, I had one of those "I could have had a V8" moments.

All of the garbage that is just a part of this kind of walk interestingly fades from my memory almost as soon as I get home, and all I can think about are the magic bits. I forget the pain and the rain and the cold and the wet and all the other nuisance factors and remember the walk for the net effect--a life-changing experience. Some hikes are better than others, but all are powerful.

And yet, at some point on every walk I find myself thinking "This is the last one of these I'm going to do. Next time I'll take the train. Or a bike, or a boat or a damn car, but I'm not walking!"

It's selective memory, I guess. It kicks in about a month or two after returning home. Once I've recovered and am back on Central Time, I'll miss that morning cappuccino, or walking through rows of olive trees, or pappardelle con cinghiale, and will start noticing sales on hiking boots and backpacks.

It's not that nuisances are simply a part of the way. I've come to understand that they are an integral part of the pleasure, that without them, there is no transformation.

Today is my first rest day on this walk along the Via Francigena, the Medieval pilgrimage route between London and Rome. I'm a week into a four-month wander from Rome northward, following roughly in he steps of Sigeric, Archbishop of Canterbury on his return home in 990ad from his investiture in Rome. The list of his stops became one of the earliest preserved documents outlining this "French route".

Not that anyone would get excited about the walk from the title of that document:

Computistical, historical and astronomical miscellany, Cotton MS Tiberius B V, part I, ff 2–73, 77–88 : 2nd quarter of the 11th century-3rd quarter of the 12th century

...is the way it's filed in the British Library. Sigeric's list (Itinerary of Archbishop Sigeric) is just that--a list of stops along his 80-day journey back to Canterbury. It is one folio that has been gathered with a list of popes, astological drawings and writings, a few prayers and poems, a map of the world.

I'm wondering what map he carried. There are several guidebooks available for this trail, but all involve too much looking down, not enough up. I prefer to trade some missed turns and trails for freedom to watch the horizon.

Thursday 1/22/15--leaving Viterbo
Bombed by a Bus, a Bath in Bagnaccio, and another Pilgrim

I got bombed by a bus in Viterbo today. It was just a water bomb, so no big deal, but it got my attention. Was walking out of town in the rain, feeling good, still dry under my little 3 euro collapsible umbrella (but with a macho print!), about to start whistling a tune, when a city bus got me good. As he skinned by me, he hit the deepest pothole in Italy and belted me with a busload of muddy water. We're talking everybody-stops-and-looks kind of drenching. It was a wet-up-to-the-bottom-of-my-hat kind of dunking. It was pointing-and-laughing kind of wet. I had to laugh myself.

Would have been a real downturn in the day except that shortly afterward I found beside my muddy trail the steaming hot spring-fed pools at Bagnaccio. These are a dozen small, shallow pools that have been shaped, cemented, and whitewashed. A small, basic little park has been built around the pools, and I could see the steam floating over the park as I slogged up the road toward the gate. After walking in a 40-degree rain for an hour or two and surviving a small bus-tsunami, the thought of a hot soak sounded great.

The water is sulphurous and strong, but it works its magic on a cold back and sore feet. I had the pool to myself for a solid hour, long enough to pickle and prune up. Felt like a new man afterwards even if it didn't make me look like one. Even the vending-machine coffee tasted great after my morning bath. It made returning to the muddy, drizzly trail a lot easier to face.

Half an hour later I looked up the road to see another hiker coming toward me. You can spot a pellegrino on the road by the typical backpack and gear and the smile. I was as surprised to see another pilgrim as he was to see me. Darius is a 20-something young guy from Rome who had taken a train up to Florence and was walking home to Rome. He told me he'd just started hiking last year but had fallen in love with it. This summer he plans to head to St. Jean Pied-de-Port to walk El Camino de Santiago. He was happy to hear that hot baths were ahead. He promised to let me know when he reached Rome, since I was the only other pilgrim he met. He said you have to be pazzo, a little crazy, to do this pilgrimage in winter...but we both were loving the day. He headed south for the baths, I marched on north toward Montefiascone.

Stopped for the night at Hotel Italia Lombardi in Montefiascone. The dome of Chiesa Santa Margherita is visible for miles to hikers from several directions. It's one of those sights, perched high on a peak as it is, that makes you think you're closer than you are. The walk in from the south, though, is interesting enough to take your mind off the distance.

This region around Lago di Bolsena is famous for having several well-preserved stretches of the original Roman roadbed that has formed a main north-south route for two thousand years. Such was the quality of the original construction that remnants of the broad paving stones are still found in the approach to Montefiascone and the road north to Bolsena. Local history says that the trails north of Montefiascone are the very ones that St. Francis of Assissi walked barefoot on his own journey to Rome in 1222.

The town surrounds a hilltop park that is the site of a former papal fortress built late in the 12th Century. The fortress was an important destination for the Popes away from Rome, and during the 14th-Century Avignon captivity, the fortress became the political center of Roman Catholic activity. The chapel that served the fortress was all but abandoned during this time, and on one visit in the early 1500s it had fallen into serious disrepair and was filled with snow. The incident earned the church he name of Santa Maria della Neve.

Friday 1/23 Bolsena

Saturday 1/24. To Acquapendente

It was a beautiful but hilly walk on the side of the north end of Lake Bolsena. Walkers could save a couple of kilometers staying down low and filling the highway, but the price of a quiet walk on gravel roads is a lot of up-and-down and a couple of thousand extra steps. San Lorenzo Nuovo is the town at the end of the lake that signals the end of that view. A market was happening today, but all it meant to me this time was a nice windbreak. I found a sunny spot on a park bench behind some market vendors and slumped into a nap like an old alley cat.

The afternoon was 8k more of road walking, but it was easy. Found a nice--but cold--room over a ristorante (Il Borgo) that liked to ration heat as many basic inns do...no radiators until after 5, or sometimes 7pm. They served a good meal, though, and after a stack of lamb chops I went to the local cinema for the dubbed Italian version of The Imitation Game. I don't really think I would have liked it better in English.

Sunday, 1/25

Radicofani was on the radar for today. It's a mountaintop town with a crenelated tower that can be seen for miles in every direction. I knew the last 10k of the day would be a hard climb, so I was glad that the first 13 were quiet and calm. Italian Sunday mornings, at least on the smaller roads I look for, are marked by little traffic and often by teams of cyclists out for a workout.

When I finally turned off the main road and headed east for the climb, the wind was noticeably stronger and colder. I didn't think about it until I was an hour into the uphill pull. The wind kept picking up until it hit 30-40mph gusts, throwing me and my backpack around at will. The wind chill was down near zero, and I wasn't prepared for that, especially since this is one of the steepest, and therefore slowest climbs of the whole trip.

It didn't help that this was one of the most scenic walks so far. I had to keep stopping, peeling gloves, and taking photos, all the time bouncing in the wind.

When I finally drug butt into Radicofani, I checked into the local community-run hostel only to find that there was no heat. The sweet volunteer that let me in assured me there was always hot water, but the heat wouldn't be on till after 5 and even then would be more of a suggestion of heat. It's not something to complain about as this hostel, like others, is run by volunteers as a service to hikers and pilgrims. The only cost to the traveler is a voluntary donation. Tonight I would gladly have paid hotel rates in exchange for a warm room, but in this small town in off season nothing was available.

A hot shower helped, though, and an hour or two in a warm local bar might be more than Sigeric and his entourage were able to find here. It's now after 5:00, I'm wrapped in a thick blanket, and stretched out on chairs pushed up to the radiator. All better. Not exactly cozy, but bearable. I have the whole hostel to myself, four bunk beds to choose from. Everyone else appears to have better sense than to climb to Radicofani today.

TEACHING "PILGRIMAGE"

It's a magical experience to walk across a country. In my experience, actual magic. A transformation occurs. Things disappear. Weights are lifted. Muscles grow. Spines stiffen. Smiles appear. Loaves and fishes are consumed, and wine is shared. And there is a price to pay for that magic.

It hurts, physically, to walk half a thousand miles. It's hard. That spine will ache. Blisters may appear. Weights are carried, and for great distances. There is pain involved, and often lots of it.

And then that magic happens. (See the first paragraph above.) Somewhere along the way, you raise your head and realize that amazing events are taking place. You become aware of the magic, and it's an easy balance--the magic is worth the pain.

That's the first key point here--there is no magic without the pain.

The second key point is that the magic is worth the pain. You don't get to the good stuff without walking through the hard stuff.

It may be one of the most difficult lessons to learn in a culture that worships ease and convenience. We love recreation, vacation, we work toward a leisurely retirement where the goal of a life seems to be to relax and go fishing.

It's also a difficult concept to teach when parents are often striving to protect their children from difficulties and hardships. We do our best to coach our young people toward better decisions that will lead them away from trials and toward successful lives.

However, it's those trials and tests that build the character necessary to thrive.

We introduce them selectively from birth, urging a child to learn to balance, to crawl, to walk, and when he falls, to get back up and try again. When the first try at riding the bike leads to a skinned knee, we encourage her to "walk it off", to get back on the bike and try again. We know the reward will be worth the effort.

Many of our parents did their best for us. They worked hard to secure a future for the family, to make sure their children "had a better life" than they did, or at least a chance at that better life.

Often, those parents wanted to protect their children from the difficulties and pain of life. Some were so intent on this that they blocked their kids from learning one of life's most important lessons--that hard work, working toward a big goal, can produce one of the greatest pleasures available in this world.

I have friends whose parents didn't want them to work during their high school years, hoping they'd have free time to enjoy that phase of life. In "protecting" them this way, though, the parents may have inadvertently delayed that part of a person's development when they learn how good it can feel to find a job, do the work, see the result, and earn those dollars and endorphins from the job well done.

And it's of course an understandable impulse. Work is hard. Life is long, if we're we're lucky. Many of those parents worked through long lives at jobs that weren't fun or fulfilling or energizing--they just put the bread on the table. It's understandable they might want to postpone for their children their entry onto the hamster wheel.

We're talking here about the ideal, however. We're doing our best to steer our students toward lives that will amaze them as well as feed them. This is where the idea of a pilgrimage enters.

Perhaps it can't be taught and must be found, accidentally encountered. It may be that I'm off the mark, but my experience tells me I'm not, that we can offer this concept to our students as we would teach any other content.

Other cultures have embraced the idea of such a trial as a rite of passage into adulthood. Some Native American tribes follow a vision quest that can be a literal trial by fire. There are Eastern cultures that practice extreme meditative ordeals that can lead one to a better place. Religions around the world embrace their members who follow a star to Mecca, or Jerusalem, Lourdes, the 88 Temples of Shikoku.

I believe we should offer to our students the idea that an Epic Journey of their choosing can be a cornerstone of a richer, happier life.

The goal itself is almost secondary. Insert your favorite "It's the journey not the goal"-type quote here.

CHANGING THE WORLD ONE SOFA AT A TIME

My buddy Kiser, his wife Pam, and I, were on a recent 2-day stopover in London when Pam's hairdryer popped a fuse in their electrical transformer. In both of their transformers, actually. Pam killed one, and then Kiser, just to make sure he had a clear picture of the situation, tested the same hairdryer in the other transformer and popped that fuse, too. Happens a lot, even with "international" hair-heating appliances. (Better just to leave them home and buy a little one there.)

As we wandered the city we kept our eyes open for electronics shops, hoping to luck into a couple of tiny fuses to repair the transformers.

On our way to a quick look at the British Museum (which is like trying to have a quick look at the Louvre or the Smithsonian), we found that New Oxford Street near Holborn tube stop is rich with electronics stores. The third one we tried had the magic fuse in stock...but only one. Kiser couldn't abandon the search for a second fuse, so we asked in shop after shop until one owner sent us to his cousin's Maplin shop two blocks up the way.

As we were homing in on a rack full of 2.5amp fuses, a tall stranger, bike helmet in hand, was asking about the same size fuses for--get this, now-- 2 blown electrical transformers. What are the odds? Seems a curling iron was involved in his blowup, too.

The stranger was almost a head taller than us and almost as garrulous as Kiser, who's never met a stranger. He democratically chats up men and women alike anywhere he goes. Much to Pam's embarrassment, he's the guy that steps up to the airport army patrol and asks him if he's keeping his machine gun oiled. Get the picture?

The Stranger grabbed the box of 10 fuses and laughed over Kiser needing them just like he did. Hearing that we were travelers, he jumped in with, "I'll buy the box, and you can have a couple of mine." Neither of us needed 10 fuses, so it was logical to split the deal. Kiser, to his credit, of course offered to pay for half a box, but the Stranger insisted.

"I'm a couchsurfer," he proclaimed proudly. Let me do you this favor, and somewhere down the road you'll pay it forward. The deal was only a 2-pound sale, so it wasn't a huge thing, but still, it was a kind gesture that tourists don't usually see from strangers in a big city. Stranger started to explain "couchsurfing", but we all assured him we knew what it was all about.

I'd been involved with Couchsurfing (with a capital C, as in the international organization) since learning of it a few years back from my buddy Audrey.

Audrey is a ferocious traveler/friend of mine from Lille, in the north of France.

I say "ferocious" because her eyesight isn't great, and yet it never keeps her from new adventures on the road. No, that's not accurate. It's not that her eyesight is simply poor...it's bad enough that she has to carry a couple of pounds of glasses, binoculars, and magnifiers just to read maps or books.

She likes movies, because the images are large enough for her to discern without her lenses. However, on the road, she's navigating through towns using a monocular for street signs and road markers. She remembers her turns in new towns by vague shapes and colors in store windows and on street corners.

All of this to say that I was surprised to hear her tell me a few years ago that on one of her recent trips down to Paris she had stayed overnight with a complete stranger, the meeting arranged through a web-organization known as Couchsurfing.org. You can imagine that it surprised me to hear that a single woman would take a chance sleeping on a stranger's sofa, but Audrey explained that the group sets up safe connections between strangers all over the world.

With more than a million members worldwide, Couchsurfing has become a goodwill phenomenon that makes perfect sense in a world becoming smaller and smaller. Members--membership in the group is free--set up profiles listing availability of a couch, a guest room, maybe floor space, or perhaps even just a willingness to meet a visitor for coffee or drive them around the town.

Strangers planning a visit to their town will select a likely-looking kindred spirit from among those profiles, email permission to "surf your couch" for a night or two. Hosts check the guest's own profile for identity, interests, and references, then accept or decline the request. No explanations are necessary.

Safeguards are in place to make sure that both surfers and hosts are who they say they are. A system of vouchers--references from established, long-term members of the association--as well as references from guests and hosts to each other are posted on profile sites. Contingency plans for easily slipping away from "surfs" that suddenly feel uncomfortable are spelled out.

Occasional problems are reported throughout the association's network, but they're very rare. In my five years with the group, I can only remember three warnings.

I first put my guest bed on the site just to see who might appear. I thought it might be a good way to meet a few people outside of my normal circle of friends. Almost immediately I had a request from a woman my age from a neighboring state. She was heading to my city of Fayetteville, Arkansas for a weekend "couch crash", a weekend-long party thrown by the local club of couchsurfers. The group plans a few days of loosely-organized pot-luck dinners, happy hours, scenic local tours, etc, and then puts out a general invitation to all regional couchsurfers to come join the fun.

That first experience convinced me that this was a group that would add to my fun quotient. Since that first visit I've entertained a New Mexico rocket scientist and his wife, a 30-something couple from Wisconsin who were wandering the country looking for a new place to plant roots, two different couples from Quebec who helped me practice my poor French, and many other folks who span a wide variety of age and interests.

And in case you're wondering, no, I've had no bad experiences. The worst that's happened has been a bit of boredom, easily solved by simply driving away to my favorite coffee shop and leaving the guests in my home. Hosts aren't required to feed or entertain. It's usually part of the fun, but there is no obligation.

I'm confident enough now in the spirit of couchsurfing that I have occasionally accepted a request, welcomed the guests, and then left the next morning on a pre-planned trip, leaving the surfers home to lock up when they depart. I like an association that attracts people I can trust this way.

After meeting our new friend in London (no names exchanged, just couchsurfing IDs) we left the store, laughing at the friendliness of the guy and reaffirming our trust in the kindness of strangers. Within an hour, a next email check-in revealed that our new buddy (code name "Beertastik") had already entered a brief, kind reference on my site.

I returned the favor, enjoying this quick exchange of bona fides that connected me once again to a like-minded person a continent away from home. The sale he shared with us was for a small amount, but the gesture was a nice slice of humanity in a busy big-city pie.

VINES, VIDEOS, CUTE CATS

Vines, youtube clips, cat videos, texts, less-than-150-character tweets, tiny books containing one quote on each page, TV segments shrinking between commercial breaks--American society is doing its dead-level best to train the focus out of us, to teach us all to forget how to concentrate. We're building a generation of mind-slaves who are locked onto phones, unable to pass between appointments without a visual guide.

And we're doing a damned fine job of it. The plan is working. Walk down the hallways of a local high school or college, and you'll find lots of faces led through those halls by a tiny screen, a culture of corpses unaware of the crowd around them. ADHD diagnoses keep a medical/pharmaceutical industry flourishing.

Students are losing the ability to focus through a single class period or to pursue long-range thought/planning.

We are losing the ability to be alone and quiet, to sit and think without electronic entertainment to amuse us. We can spend hours hypnotized by devices, and at the end of those hours care little about what we've just seen.

In a recent music history class we were discussing the scope of Medieval cathedrals in Europe--building projects that spanned one hundred years or more. I was struck then by the contrast between hundred-year thoughts and our 21st Century "ideal" of 30-second video bursts. It's a comparison that leaves me a little sad.

Focus on a long-term plan takes practice. If we don't broach the idea in school, where will it happen?

JOURNAL, WEEK 3-4

Monday, 26 January

If you're looking for a place to get out of the cold for an evening and can afford the price, an Italian ristorante in Radicofani is a good place to start. When I checked into the community hostel on this January afternoon, a volunteer named Gerasmundo recommended the Ristorante La Grotta...which was a good thing as it was the only place open on a Sunday night in Radicofani. Imagine a picture of a traditional old Italian restaurant, and this would fit...a bar up front, and in the back a long room of tables under a stone barrel-vaulted ceiling. Racks of wine bottles and vases of flowers lined the walls.

I huddled in a back corner, blissfully warm and welcomed by a friendly server, Lalia. When she figured me for a pellegrino, she brought me a house bottle of their own Sangiovese red, a basket of bread, and told me to take all the time I wanted. I had planned to do my Jabba the Hut act, order one of everything on the menu to have an excuse to stay in the womb a little longer, but Lalia told me I didn't have to.

Half the tables filled while I was there, and Lalia knew every customer. She joined most at their tables at least once during the night, swapping stories as she took orders.

She brought me a tureen of mushroom zuppe and a big

basket of chunks of toasted bread for croutons. Following that was a platter of creamed potatoes covered with roasted cinghiale, local wild boar, in a rich red wine gravy. I made it respectably through those two courses before giving up. Other patrons around me didn't seem to have any trouble working through a secondo main course with side dishes and then dessert. A coffee and a local amaro did me for the night.

When my head started dropping, I figured it was time to make my move. I shuffled across the lane, climbed the two flights (final climbing for the day!) to the hostel, piled the blankets from all four bunks onto mine, and crawled into my bag. Amaro dreams of old friends returned to life and strange wild animals seemed about right for this night.

Monday, 1/26/15

I knew it would be a cold shock crawling out of the nest of blankets this morning, and sure enough, it was. I've really been spoiled to having heat when I want it and a place to get warm whenever needed. I'm not sure I can fathom the constitution of Northerners who thrive on the cold. Doesn't work for me. Nothing to be done but get up and go, so I did.

The temperature was right at freezing this morning, and the wind was a steady 15-20 mph. For a Texas boy, that's kind of a bitter way to start the day. The good news, though, was that I was headed downhill after climbing all that way yesterday. The sky was bitingly blue, so I snapped a few last photos of Radicofani and shuffled down the mountain. I was hoping to find a place to stop early for the night and recover some core heat, but I didn't expect to get lucky. San Quirico D'Orcia was about 30k to the north and the first place I was pretty sure to find space. Sure enough, that's where the day took me.

It was an interesting day for wildlife...more birds than normal and in great numbers, a badger finishing the night's work, and a deer that I spooked from his hide beside the road. I'm used to white tailed deer flicking a white flag as they run from you, but this Italian version had a double puff on her backside, big as a couple of throw pillows.

My last muddy adventure of the day came as I decided to try a shortcut shown on one of my trail maps. Most of these don't really turn out to be any shorter, but this one had possibilities...a straight shot down a country lane, across a bridge clearly marked on the map, and I might cut off a couple of kilometers. All went well until that well-marked bridge, which...well, which wasn't. I could see where a bridge used to be, but that didn't get me a dry path across the water. A spotty trail of stones had been pitched by hikers to form most of a path through the shallow rapids. I did my part, adding a dozen more stones in open spots, then boldy step across. And boldly slipped off 2/3 of the way across and went in up to my knees. I was only 4k away from hot shower when I filled up both boots with cold river. Brilliant way to stage a triumphal entry into San Quirico D'Orcia.

Tuesday, 1/27/15

To Buonconvento

I almost slept through this day. I was whipped from a couple of freezing, windy days with lots of climbs, and ready for a rest day. I'd arrived late yesterday in San Quirico D'Orcia and crashed. Got up in time for a walk around the centro storico, but didn't have the energy to give the city it's due. After an early dinner of a bad Italian imitation of a hamburger, I spent the evening in my room--get this--sewing a new zipper into my hiking pants. That's right--I blew a zipper. Nothing exciting, just broke what was not supposed to be easy to break. (What was exciting was going into a sewing shop and trying to describe to the sweet lady in the shop what I needed by using gestures. Didn't get arrested, though, and I left with a zipper.)

Anyway, when I woke this morning and saw the sun shine yet again, I knew I should walk while the walking is good. It was better than good...it was perfect. Sunny, 35F, and no wind, it was a perfect day to walk down off of San Quirico's mountaintop Torrenieri and then Buonconvento. The Tuscan countryside put on a show today, and I was happy I was there to see it.

By the way, if you have a few days in the hills just south of Siena, those three towns are worth a stop and a stroll.

Tonight, dinner at Albergo Roma and maybe a movie-- American Sniper. I'd like to see it before the Oscars, but I'm not sure it's worth staying up late and dozing through another film when my less-than-brilliant language skills fail me.

Wednesday, 1/28/15

Made it to Monteroni D'Arbia today, 20k or so. Rather than look for a place to stay here, I bused the 15k on into Siena to a little place I know near Il Campo, Piccolo Hotel Etruria. It's basic, but cheap, and it's only a few feet off the Piazza. Tomorrow I'll train back out to Monteroni and finish walking into the city. (Part of my OCD at work...wanting to have covered the entire distance on foot.).

Siena is as impressive as ever, but largely empty of the summer crowds I'm used to seeing. Walking into Piazza Del Campo on a sunny winter day, though, is still magical. The circle of buildings that guard the center are an effective wind break, and it's as if I've stepped from a refrigerator into an oven. The sparse crowd are all faces turned to soak up the sun, the younger bunches sprawled on the pavement as if it's summer. Step back into the shadows and there's an immediate drop of ten degrees, but stay in the sun, and...well, just stay in the sun. That's what it's for.

Thursday, 1/29/15

An 8am train out to Monteroni for a cold walk into the city under a thick gray sky. A heavy front is edging down, bringing more winter with it. It's almost February, so this is expected. I'll sit out the worst of it here in Siena and try to get a little work done.

A memory:
I'd forgotten about cheap hotels in cities. I don't think it matters what country...I've had this experience in several--the surprise of middle-of-the-night drama. This time it was a loud one-act play staged on the stairs in

the hallway of Piccolo Hotel Etruria at 3:30am. Through the haze of sleep and another language I missed the backstory. What I got from the tone--what everyone in the hotel heard--was, He: anger. She: weeping, wailing, loudly. He: more anger...I thought he might hit her. She: pleading, more crying, explaining. He: dissolving into a bit of pleading of his own.

Scene change: shift, stomping, up one flight of stairs. She: rising voice, angry now. He: frantic explaining, justifying. She: shouting.

(I'm wondering if anyone in management at the hotel is hearing this and will intervene. Then I remember...there probably isn't any staff in the building after midnight. Cheap hotel in a big city.)

Finale--Both: voices lowered in volume, emotion. They're still on the stairs, apparently, not ready to take the drama backstage. Tone changes to conversational, and then quiet laughter. All is resolved. Happily ever after...or for the rest of tonight, anyway.

Thank you, and good night. Catch our next performance tomorrow night same time, probably same location...cheap hotel in a big city.

Cheap hotel postscript
    Or
Act Two, following night. 10pm

I'm about to fall asleep when I hear someone moving furniture nearby. Repeatedly. Then I realize it's actually someone snoring ...someone snoring so loudly that I could hear them in another room. Now, this isn't an adjacent room, this was from clear across the hallway. At first I ignored it, but then I finally had to open the door to see where it was coming from. A guy is sitting on the bench at the end of the hallway, his head between his knees, snoring like a two-stroke Evinrude running low on gas. When I closed the door, he woke for a minute, then he was right back at it. When I went to sleep, he was still out there. About an hour later I hear more loud talking from the hallway, and it's the police who have come to sort him out. I never heard if he'd just lost his way to his room or decided that the corridor was good enough.

A thought:
Old episodes of Knight Rider, Walker Texas Ranger, and yes, Love Boat, have even less luster dubbed in Italian.

Friday, 1/30/15

SIGERIC made his journey in 990ad. Today in Siena, I happened into the tiny Chiesa San Pietro on Via Montanini. According to documents in the church, it is from the same time period as that...first mentioned in a historic record in 998. It's interesting to think that this structure--the roots of it, at least--that now watches shoppers and Mopeds and Fiats buzz by once was a sanctuary for pilgrims of a different era. Imagine during the past thousand years how many different lives have passed through the building, how many rulers, soldiers and saints, armies and angels and pilgrims have wandered past its doors.

A fun gift of s surprise snowstorm tonight. I almost slept through it but woke in time to run out to the Campo for photos. I'd never seen Siena in snow before.

Saturday, 1/31/15

And I got to see a little more snow his morning! More than I wanted, actually. The sun was shining when I marched out of Piccolo Hotel Etruria this morning, so I didn't wrap up the bag well. I was barely on the edge of the city when the rain came and came fast...mixed with sleet and snow and then more cold rain. Like an ijit, I made my situation worse trying to dig out my little waterproof Fuji point-and-shoot so that I could "capture the moment". The moment turned out to be a wet mess. My poncho, my "impermiabile", isn't. I have to find a can of spray to see if I can make it at least a bit waterproof.

One funny thing happened before the rain. I stopped for a quick coffee at Charlie Bar on the north end of Siena. On the wall there is their certificate from the Guiness folks (the records, not the beer) confirming that one of their bar guys, Aldinucci Riccardo, set the world record last May by making 322 cappuccinos in an hour. That's a lotsa cappuccini!

I'm one of very few people tonight in Monteriggioni, another--gasp--walled town north of Siena. The old walls and turrets (begun in the 1200s) are largely intact. The signs claim that the fortress was inpenetrable except for one war in the 1530s when Florentine armies bombarded them into submission.

I'm in a nice hostel, one of only a couple of places to stay, but once again, little heat. I'm in search of a warm bar/cafe.

Sunday, 2/1/15. FEBRUARY!!

I found one, but got thrown out at closing time, 7pm. It was kind of a long evening wrapped up in a blanket with my back tot the radiator in the hostel.

Had a chat with Christian, the only other occupant in the rooms. He works for a travel agency and has seen a lot of the world for a 30-something guy. As I was leaving town this morning, I bumped into Koster, the man who had checked me into the hostel yesterday. He was headed into a bar down the hill from the old town and insisted I stop in a have a coffee with him. Nothing big, just the normal Italian stand-at-the-bar-and-chug-chug-it thing. It was a nice way to start the day.

And the weather held! Beautiful walk to San Gimignano, although I'm pulling up a little lame with a bad muscle in my thigh. The leg was really complaining as I climbed the last hills into the city.

It was interesting to get there early on a Sunday afternoon...the city was as empty as I have ever seen it. After a shower and a quick snooze, though I stuck my head back out into the street and was almost run down by a parade float full of Smurfs. Carnevale had begun in San Gimignano!

This version comes complete with a few large floats full of Italian cartoon characters, a DJ pumping tunes, and a town full of little kids in costume spraying silly string and chunking mounds of paper confetti on any and all spectators.

Monday, Groundhog Day

Another beautiful day to walk. I made decent time to Castelfiorentina but had to keep looking back over my shoulder at the sunrise around San Gimignano. I pulled up lame, though--there's some fire in my right quad that's not supposed to be there. I thought I could walk it off, but it's getting worse.

Glad the cameras weren't out watching me. I wouldn't want a record of that sight--me, trying to vary my stride and pace somehow to take the strain off that leg. When I walked backwards (for photographic reasons, you know), it didn't hurt, so I tried that now and then. If I lifted that right foot like a trotter, it helped, so that got into the mix...kind of like half of an 8-to-5 march step. If I slowed way down and walked like I was trying not to wake the baby, that seemed to make a difference, too. But the whole mixture of those efforts came out looking like some perverted line dance, or maybe a Bruno Mars-with-a-humpback video.

Stumbled into the Hotel Lami in the main piazza at Castelfiorentino. It's nicer than I can afford, but I can rationalize the expense with the need to get off my leg. The sweet Nona who's running the place was also nice enough to let me into her kitchen, too, for a quick photo. The building is 300 years old, and the big cuccina features an open fire place that's countertop height with a wide brick chimney/vent. Nona had a small fire of sticks glowing there, right next to her gas stovetop that shares the vent. She has a gas oven beside the stove but says she like cooking on the open fire. There's a long table in the center of the room that obviously serves as the real living room for her family. While I had my breakfast in the hotel's small dining room this morning, I could hear her daughter and grandkids stopping by for coffee and biscotti on their way to school.

Tuesday, 2/3/15

Still have lots of miles to go, so I'll stop at Empoli for a couple of days and see if that will help. The rain is coming anyway, so I may as well be indoors working and resting instead of totin' the big pack out on the road. The extra weight of the pack is the problem.

Nicolo', at the desk of the Hotel Sole in Empoli, is working hard on his English and promised to correct my Italian. (He doesn't know what he's in for.). I reckon I'll fix 'im up with some by-god Tex-Arkansan vocab that will do 'im right when 'Mercans come to visit.

Went to the movies tonight. Only two choices, and both looked bad, but I was tired of sitting and writing. Went for Night at the Museum...the 4th or 5th, whatever. It looked pretty dull in English, and it was only a little less dull dubbed in Italian. Worth the time to practice listening, but I also caught up on more sleep, too.

Wednesday, 2/4/15

Rest day in Empoli, just relaxing and trying to stay off the leg. Tomorrow to San Miniato and Fucecchio.

Thursday, 2/5/15

It was a wet walk to Fucecchio today, but thankfully, a

short one. Only 13k today (My days are getting shorter!), and the temp stayed near 45F...could have been miserable if it were colder. The way was narrow, though, with traffic on the road all the way. Not a pleasant day of walking.

What made it more bearable is the Hotel Campagnola I checked into at the end of the walk. I'd intended to make it to Ponte a Cappiano, but in the end, I didn't want to think about a cold hostel, even one as interesting as the Ostello on the Ponte de' Medici. The Campagnola offered hot water and even heat in the room, so I indulged.

Salvatore, the extra-happy hotelier, seemed extra-extra-happy to have an American staying in the hotel, breaking into the first phrase of the national anthem-- ours, not theirs--each time I walked in the door.

The hostel that I didn't quite reach--the modern version-- is in a bridge house built over the River Usciana, a branch of the Arno. The original toll house was destroyed during a war between Lucca and Florence, then later rebuilt by Florence as a more fortified structure to control River traffic.

The rebuilt bridge house was included later in a set of drawings by Leonardo da Vinci of fortifications in the area. Reproductions of his designs at what is now the hostel (men on one side of the bridge lane, women in the other), show a set of locks and a small defendable structure that would "allow for the fishing of eels" as well as some control over flooding and drainage of the swamps at nearby Fucecchio. In pleasant weather it's one of the most special hostels on the Via Francigena.

Friday, 2/6/15
Altopascio
I GOT KISSED TODAY
   Or
SPREADING THE PELLEGRINO LOVE

His name is Giovanni. He's a nice enough guy, but I'm not sure it's going anywhere.

The forecast said rain today, so I'd planned to sit it out. When I woke up today, that had changed to cloudy, so I decided to walk. By the time breakfast was done, it had changed again to showers, but I was committed.

I headed north back over the bridge and up a hill that gave a nice view of the morning sun on the snow atop the Apennines. I'm heading in that general direction but have another week of walking on coastal flats before I'm back up in the mountains.

After an hour of quiet, beautiful lanes, my route joined one with more traffic. I was still rubber-necking my way along the road when a man in a Peugot transit van stopped and waved me over to his side of the road.

"Pellegrino", he called as I walked up, then grabbed me by the shoulders for quick baci, the Italian kiss on both cheeks. It was clear that the guy was a pilgrim at heart himself, so I didn't take his advances too personally.

Giovanni told me he was indeed a pellegrino and had been out working on the Francigena today, posting the little mini-bumper-sticker signs that mark the trail. He wanted to make sure I knew I wasn't on the "real" Via Francigena, and I was finally able to assure him I wasn't lost.

The concept of a single Francigena route is a bit simplistic. At any point along the way there may be three or four variants, for bikes, for routes through the woods, for ways along roads, and sometimes because someone has started a new hostel and wants to reroute the trail by his front door.

It was fun speaking with Giovanni as he had been working on parts of the route I'd just walked. He's one of a host of volunteers who give their time to find suitable, safe ways for hikers to walk, mark the trails, and occasionally build paths that will allow walkers to avoid walking near traffic.

Coming down the mountain from Radicofani ten days ago I had been surprised to find one of these byways newly built beside a particularly curvy mountainous highway. It was a welcome relief from dodging cars on a narrow two-lane road with no shoulder. I mentioned it to my new friend, and he was happy that someone had noticed. He had been one of the workers who helped build the path.

It's interesting that membership in this society of walkers and riders conveys instant friendship. A few years back I was walking part of this pilgrimage when I came around a corner and saw a young couple with backpacks at a picnic table beside the road. I waved and walked over, and the same greetings happened. The couple was from Martigny, up in the southern edge of Switzerland, and they were hiking the Francigena down to Rome. I later learned from them that I was the only other pilgrim they met during their month on the road.

Giovanni was happy to bump into another pilgrim during the off season that he wanted to give me the rundown on advice for the best places to walk and to sleep on the next few stops heading north. He gave me a souvenir Via Francigena sign and a few more hugs and kisses before he headed on down the road and I commenced to dodging traffic again.

Just a kilometer farther, though, I came to another of his roadside paths and was happy again to take advantage of his work.

Pilgrims who have walked the Camino de Santiago will remember that the entire 500 miles of that route through Spain has been developed bit by bit until now hikers rarely have to share pavement with cars. Italy isn't there yet, but there are signs that work is headed in that direction.

As Giovanni drove away, he honked and waved another of his Francigena signs at me, our version of a not-so-secret fraternity handshake.

Saturday, 2/7/15
LUCCA KEPT ITS WALLS

Walked from Altopascio into Lucca today. While other fortified cities gradually let go of the walls around their city centers, Lucca managed to keep its spectacular star-shaped walls intact. The great mound surrounding the inner city is now a living organism of culture for the town, busy with walkers, runners, lovers, concerts, and of course, history. The top of the ramparts is wide enough that for a time the loop around the city was used for car races. Now it provides views of the outer city and in the distance, the snow-topped Apennines.

The city claims as one of its own the composer Giacomo Puccini. His childhood home is a museum near the ornate Chiesa San Michele Del Foro. A bronze of a seated Puccini kept watch today over a piazza filled with booths in a local art show today. Weekly performances of his music are scheduled throughout the year. Every Friday night, 7pm, year-round, patrons can find a performance of Puccini arias in a local church, and his operas are frequently staged to satisfy the demand of fans visiting the city.

Sunday, 2/8/15
WALKING LESSONS—Bozzano

Still having some leg trouble that started back before Groundhog Day. Usually on these walks it's a toe, first. It starts rubbing on part of your boot until it's really sore. You have to find a way to walk on a different part of your foot to ease the pressure on that toe.

If you're walking in hot weather or you're just unlucky, you rub a blister on one of your feet, and you find a way to lean just right when you step to get some of the weight off that part of your foot.

The summer before I left on this trip I pulled something on the inside of my left knee, enough so that I had to just stay off the leg for awhile. I'd been doing wind sprints...OK, I'd been doing an old lazy guy's version of wind sprints and stretched something there I shouldn't have stretched. It was really slow healing, and I began to think it might be enough to stop me on this walk.

That problem hasn't surfaced on this trip, but another one has. I've ripped a muscle in my right quad. (I know, it's probably not exactly that, but it sounds better than saying "Mommy, it hurts when I do this."). It's the kind of pain I expect to just slow down a little and limp to make it go away, but so far that's not working.

I mentioned before efforts to adjust my stride to ease the worry. Today I noticed that if I swivel my hip to bring that right leg forward, kind of like swinging a dead weight to the front, that also helps. Now I'm starting to get sore on my left side in my calf and knee from all the swivel-hipped marching. Haven't figured out yet how to fix that, but I think it's going to involve drugs or pirouettes. Or both.

CRITICAL THINKING EXERCISE:--PILGRIMAGE and ART

This is a "connection" exercise, one that asks students to look for connections between several seemingly unrelated ideas.

1) Begin by asking students to define 'pilgrimage'.

2) After they've had a few minutes to think and write, ask them to define 'art'.

3) As a backdrop to their thinking/writing, you might offer examples of some Spanish (Galician) music like they might hear on the Camino de Santiago.

4) At this point introduce the concept of El Camino de Santiago, its history and current practice.

5) Another connection—breakup stories. Ask students to think about relationships and their endings—a funny one, sad one, whatever. (You are setting the stage for a "pilgrimage breakup"—Marina Abramovic and Ulay, THE LOVERS, THE GREAT WALL WALK.)

6) To offer some background on these two artists' performance art, show some quick clips and stills of their more challenging art concepts.

7) Show students a map/photos/video of the Great Wall. Give them some concept of the length and scope of the wall.

8) Share bits of the video of THE LOVERS, THE GREAT WALL WALK.

9) Ask students to a] think for 2 minutes--any thoughts, impressions, connections from the work, particularly whether this project fits their definitions of the word "pilgrimage", then b] to write for 10minutes about those thoughts.

10) If time permits, you might want to show a followup to THE LOVERS.   There is a touching video of the reunion of the two artists some years after their Great Wall walk during Marina Abramovic's retrospective piece, THE ARTIST IS PRESENT. It is easily found on youtube and features a surprise visit by Ulay while Abramovic was performing her work at MOMA.

11) As a final step, you might want to invite students to spend extra time outside of class considering the subject, to write further if they're so moved and then to submit online. Any responses judged worthy may warrant an extra credit point.

SCENES FROM THE SEASIDE--FROGS AND COFFEE AT CIVITAVECCHIA

Cafe Chalet Garibaldi, Civitavecchia, Italy

The train station in Civitavecchia is only a hundred yards or so from the water's edge, a situation that helped this town grow into the "Sunday resort" for residents of Rome. Since unification in the 1870's, summer heat has driven city dwellers to hop a train for the hour-long ride out from Trastevere to the string of cafes and umbrella renters that welcome them to the shore. The stone fortress now apparently guards only the pier where gigantic cruise ships offload their tonnage of tourists every day of the week.

Sitting in the shade of a cool veranda at the Chalet Garibaldi, I'm eavesdropping on two twenty-something couples at the next table. A dark-skinned girl with a Brit/Indian accent holds forth on the bad manners of one of their friends the night before who had been chasing an underaged girl. The guy with her sits quietly, either introverted or missing the English or just bored. The other woman is American and chimes in occasionally in a chirpy schoolgirl voice; then she returns to making out with her Italian guy. They're enthusiastic, like they just discovered how juicy a kiss can be. Tongues are involved; inhibitions are not. When they come up for air, he lights a cigarette, doing his best to look cool at it. Like every other smoker here, though, his face scrunches into a squinting grimace every time he takes a puff.

They're interrupted by an African man their own age who stops and stands beside their table with a small djembe, a stick ringed with bright leather bracelets, a dozen sunglasses, and a wooden frog that he strokes with a stick to make it croak. The group waves him away; he calmly walks on, humming softly, knowing it was a long shot. He doesn't seem concerned, apparently confident that if he's pleasant and croaks that frog enough times, someone will buy one...maybe just to get him to stop with the noise already. He circles the terrazza, then returns to his stool at the open-air bar, resumes his chat with the bartender right where they left off.

Two gray-hairs at another table ignore the long-empty cups on their table and swap words and gestures. They speak softly but seriously, which means lots of waving and pointing and other manual punctuation. (Italian language generally isn't taught with accompanying hand signs, but it should be.) The men work their way through the morning's news, popping solutions for a string of issues...the "crisis", immigration, Berlusconi, the FIFA scandal, weather...wait--there's more on Berlusconi, accompanied by a smirking laugh.

A young couple sits near me for a coffee, and immediately her phone rings. She sings to it, "Pronto...Ciaociaociao! Tesoro, Tesoro, Cara mia!" Then she spits out a rap faster than any pro, sounding like snare sticks on a hard board, followed by"Certo! A dopo...baci, baci, baci, ciaociaociaociao!" Picks up a crust of a croissant and munches away.

Two more senior men struggle stiffly into chairs in the middle of the terrace, wait for a server, wave off the Sunglass Kid, then pull out their cellphones. Just like addicted teenagers, they ignore each other and stare at their cell screens. Unlike kids, though, their eyes can't quite handle the little screens. They squint and shift, pump them like weights, trying to find a distance that focuses. The cute young brunette server stops at their table, gives them their usual thirty seconds of flirt time, throws a sarcastic comeback over her shoulder as she leaves to get their drinks. Two one-euro coffees will buy them an hour or two table rental.

Five twenty-year-old boys land at a corner table, half in shade and half in the sun. The pavement is warming up, but the breeze still makes the shady tables feel like paradise on a Friday morning. The five order orange Fantas and light their hand-rolled cigarettes. (Remember the crisis? It's getting harder to afford store-bought cigarettes.) All five in unison have a puff, a sip, and then start pumping a leg nervously under the table. Out come the phones, and the heads drop in prayer to Lord Apple. "Our Father, who art an iPhone 6, hallowed be thine apps..."

While the table scenes progress, the pit orchestra at the bar has been sawing away. Within ten minutes, twenty players have walked in, stirred their sugar packet with the tiny spoon good for little else, slurped the jigger of espresso in two gulps, then surged out singing, "Ciao, Grazie! Ciaociao." A few make the play with hardly a pause in their step...the bar dude sees them coming, slides the cup to meet them with impressive precision, they suck it down on the rebound, then use the bounceback off the marble counter to take them right out the door. It's coffee efficiency at its finest, practiced by professionals, in a country that perfected the art. (Kids, don't try this at home.)

One of the cooks from the bar comes over trailing a babbling Brit lady. She asks me if I speak English...the Brit is concerned about something, and the cafe lady can't decipher what it is she needs. Ms. Brit explained that she and her husband had stopped here for lunch on their way to a B&B down the street. She's very concerned about letting the host know what time they'll arrive and has been asking this woman to call and speak to the B&B people for her. She's afraid they'll lose their room. (It's noon-fifteen.) I checked the map, and the place is perhaps all of 200 yards away from the cafe. She could have walked down and knocked on the door in the time it took for this conversation, and I suggested that it might be easier to do this. She's in a kerfuffle, though, and nothing will do but that the cafe lady call for her. Rather than push back against the British Empire, the woman rolls her eyes and calls...and gets a recording.

That's her sign to exit, and I'm left attending to the tourist. She decides to go looking for a different cafe with WIFI so that she can email the B&B. That's my sign to wish her well and sit back down to my lunch. I watch her walk back to her table, and I see her husband sitting there, reading a paper, totally unconcerned and uninterested. He's lived through this storm before and knows just how to wield his umbrella.

The five guys' heads are still down. Two of them have now inserted headphones into various orifices, and the leg pumping takes on a rhythmic bump.

An elderly British couple fresh off a cruise ship, shuffles up and drops into empty chairs, then order tea. Of course. The palm trees wave at them, agreeing that Earl Grey isn't a bad idea on a nice Friday morning in June.

Two more street vendors invade, and Sunglasses decides he's milked this cow dry. He drains his own cup, slides off the stool, and saunters down the plaza, smiling, humming, croaking.

I FELL ASLEEP IN THE PIAZZA TODAY

I fell asleep in the piazza today. Again. It's getting to be a habit, and I'm not proud.

I was on a rest day. It was noon-thirty, the air was cool, but the sun was out. The day before I had survived another day's walk and discovered this sunny square. I had my shower, and wandered into a beautifully warm, inviting, sunlit piazza, complete with a white marble statue of some unknown-to-me liberating Italian or maybe another Cristoforo Colombo. I joined the other lunchers there (mostly awake), leaned back on the warm stone, and promptly dozed off like a toothless old bear in the zoo.

Today I'm back there in the same square, catching up on my rest...and dozing off again. I'd barely sat down before I was out cold.

When I woke up thirty minutes later (after spending that half hour nodding and jerking like a George Brett bobble-head doll), I was all alone. Except, of course, for the homeless guy who was taking a break from sitting on the sidewalk jiggling his cup of coins to come sit in the sun beside me.

He and I have a nodding acquaintance now. He's around my age--in his fifth or sixth decade, anyway. I saw him out yesterday in his maroon windbreaker, gray trousers, and worn purple crocs. He apparently spends most of the day kneeling, hands clasped as if in prayer, a cup or hat to catch coins placed in front of him, hardly making eye contact with passers-by, never pushy, but regular and persistent in the hours he keeps.

And I'm wondering if passers-by at my piazza today are starting to group me with prayer-guy? "Yeah...the old toothless-bear dude who falls asleep on the statue of Garibaldi after lunch!" I'm not sure that's the legend I want on my tombstone...but then, I guess there are worse ones.

After my little power nap in the piazza, I found the strength to head back to my room for a proper rest.

Today after a couple of carefully-spaced sleeps before and after lunch, I headed to Piazza Roma next to just south of my room (different piazza, different liberator, same sun) to do a little homework with my Italian phrase book. It didn't take long, though, before...well...more nodding and bobbing, and this time I think there was snorting and snoring involved. But, come on...Italian prepositions. I mean, really--they're enough to make anyone go cross-eyed.

A new Venezuelan friend I met along the way went with me to a movie tonight. MARIGOLD HOTEL is a sweet, if a bit predictable, film, with beautiful scenes of beautiful Indian people and the countryside. We both enjoyed the movie and the music. After my friend headed back to her room, though, I stopped off at my favorite little bar, Cafe' Touche', for a jigger of grappa. The barista there is trying to expand my taste in the stuff, but so far it all taste pretty much like lighter fluid to me.

At the moment I'm stuck on a digestive called Nonino, a drier version of an Amaro. Not sure I could tell a wetter version from the dry, but who cares? What I like is sitting under the plastic shelter over the cafe's terraza, sipping that clear magic, feeling my head react immediately. (Gravity is an interesting thing, isn't it? The way some liquids can flow uphill from your mouth directly to your brain?)

It was also interesting to me to discover last night that I was staring down into my Nonino with my eyes closed. Again. Did it again. How many times does that make today? I've lost count, but I may have to start paying attention. It's now the following morning, time to walk again, but I'm a little bit drowsy...

JOURNAL, WEEK 5-6

Monday, 2/9/15—Viareggio

There's a point on the curvy, hilly road between Lucca and Al Sasso where the pavement suddenly leans the other way, toward the coastline instead of inland. If you're not walking or pumping a bicycle like lots of guys were yesterday, you won't notice it, maybe. If you are on your feet, though, it feels great to reach that point after a hard climb.

It's even nicer half a kilometer farther along when you see the little town of Al Sasso peek through the trees. It's backed by a view of the Ligurian Sea and the delta-like flats of the Lago di Massaciuccoli that spills into the sea near Viareggio.

The remains of the first two Sundays of Viareggio Carnevale are blowing through the streets and floating on the canals around the city. It's a big draw here, and they stretch out the celebration to five weekends, culminating with a nighttime masquerade/parade and fireworks display on the 28th of February. Store windows and markets are sporting bigger-than-life papier mâché figures, and balconies are decorated with flags and streamers and masks.

I walked into town on some quiet gravel roads that border the lake. It was on the west end of this lake that Puccini lived in his Torre Del Lago home. This was after he had "made it" and had begun to be recognized as one of the leading opera composers of the end of the 19th Century.

Last night after walking the long pier into the bay at Viareggio, I stumbled onto the piazza that honors the British poet P. B. Shelley and the cafe by that name. I sipped my Amaro Nonino and read about the last days of Shelley's life.

He and his second wife, Mary Shelley, kept a house in Lerici, just north of here. He was sailing home in his small boat, the Don Juan, when he was caught in a sudden violent storm and drowned. His body wasn't recovered until nine days later when it washed ashore near La Spezia. Shelley was cremated here, and there are engravings of the open funeral pyre.

He was just a few weeks shy of his thirtieth birthday when he died. According to an article by Stacy Conradt in Mental Floss, Shelley's widow kept his heart, which had not burned away in the funeral fire, and carried it with her for the rest of her life.

Connections occur all along the Via Francigena, and the bust of Shelley in the piazza that honors him reminds me of another up the road. If I can make it over the Alps at the northern border of Italy, I'll follow the Francigena route down into the "Swiss Riviera" at Montreux and Lausanne. This part of Lac Leman/Lake Geneva has been an inspiration to artists, writers, composers, for many generations. Hindemith and Stravinsky are two of the most famous composers who worked there for a time. Montreux is still the site of one of the most famous jazz festivals in the world.

It was on the north side of Lac Leman that the Shelleys, Lord Byron, and Byron's doctor/friend kept homes the summer of 1816. From high up the side of those foothills of the Jura Mountains, you can watch the storms cross the southern shore at Evian and boil their way across the lake, shooting lightning bolts as they come. Perhaps it was one of those storms that inspired Mary Shelley to write Frankenstein in that home. There is a picturesque Medieval castle at the east end of the lake, and Byron is famous in the area for his poem The Prisoner of Chillon, inspired by his visit to the dungeons there. (He's also a little bit infamous for a bit of graffiti-- he carved his name into a pillar in the dungeon. But that's another story.)

Tuesday, 2/10/15 Viareggio to Pietrasanta (stayed in Viareggio)

It was great walking a long, flat, straight road by the sea this morning. The Lungomare from Viareggio toward Pietrasanta is lined with shops, cafes, parks, and Palm trees. This morning it sports a few walkers, some joggers, and a dog that looks like a sheep dog with dreadlocks. I walked the lazy route to Pietrsanta, spent a few minutes in the piazza near the stations, then trained back to the hotel in Viareggio.

Dinner tonight was off the side of the fishboat again--a tray of crab crochettes...small breaded bits of crab and potatoes, deep fried. Dessert is a cup of thick cioccolatta caldo con panna at the Libreria Mondavi, a bookstore cafe that this month features a giant carnevale head out front.

Wednesday, 2/11/15 Pietrasanta to Marina di Massa

Shifted my hotel to Hotel Roma at Marina di Massa today, then walked the stretch to cover the distance. It was another perfect, sunny day alongside the shore.

Thursday, 2/12/15 Massa to Sarzana (stayed in Marina di Massa)

Since the hotel is an easy one, I left the big pack there today and hiked another 15k or so up to Sarzana. The way took me along the shore near Carrara, beside marble yards filled with huge blocks waiting shipment. Flatbed trucks loaded with future works of art (or someone's Carrara countertops) passed me constantly.

I had coffee at a sunny cafe across the street from a park at Marina di Carrara. I'd just finished a cup, or else I would have stopped again down the street when I came to a diner sporting the famous golden arches...only these were for McLouis's Diner, a blatant copy of McD's, but tucked away far enough from American trademark attorneys that no one cared.

Friday, 2/13/15 Walked Sarzana to Aulla; train for weekend off to Vernazza

I was ready for a real day off, but the sun was shining today, and rain is predicted for tomorrow. I decided to push ahead to Aulla and then rest through the rain.

Sarzana to Aulla involves a steep, beautiful climb out of the coastal flats up into the hills. At the foot of the marble mountains. I climb up to Brina, the ruins of an old fortress, and was sucking air when I heard the clatter of walking sticks. A hiker came down from above me, wearing a bright green safety vest. Giovanni, an avid local hiker and volunteer on the local mountain rescue team, stopped to check on me (I told you I was sucking air) and to chat about trails in the area. It was nice to bump into a friendly face on the side of the mountain.

I huffed on up into the stratosphere, hoping for a cup of coffee at Ponzano Superiore. It's an "unknown" Tuscan hill town that is as picturesque as many others, yet still remains off the tourist radar. One reason may be that there's no place for a coffee there. I trailed on down to the state road, jousted with traffic the rest of the way to Aulla, and discovered an easy train connection from there to the Cinque Terre. Rather than take my break in Aulla, I headed to Vernazza, an easy hour away to take the weekend on the coast.

Friday night in Vernazza turned out to be a quiet time in the off season...not even a bar open for dinner. Fortunately, I was too tired to care. I found a room (Ivo Camere), about 70 flights of stairs straight up, and crashed.

Saturday, 2/14/15 Day off. Vernazza to Manarola to Riomaggiore

Sure enough, the predicted drizzle started in Vernazza and continued today. I decided to shift to Manarola and walk on around to Riomaggiore, the southernmost of the five towns. When I stepped off the train in Manarola, I found the low, paved walkway--the Via Dell'Amore--that runs just above the sea to Riomaggiore, was closed due to some dangerous rock slides. I settled for another short train ride and found a room at Hotel La Zorza in the middle of the Main Street. Sylvia ran the one-woman show there. She said that during the off season it was so slow that one person and her cleaning woman could handle the business.

After a lazy day, I discovered again that nothing was open for dinner that night. However, La Spezia, an industrial city on the eastern side of the mountain, is only a 10-minute, $2 train ride away. I found life there, along with a really mediocre burger, and a short ride back "home".

Sunday, 2/15/15. Day off in Riomaggiore

It was great to sleep a few minutes later, have a slow breakfast set out by Sylvia, and then catch up on some work. When the sun peeked out, I wandered a bit, took some photos, and then returned to working hard at relaxing. After watching the local kids in costumes for their small-town Carnevale party, I took another early train into La Spezia for the afternoon. The boat basin there sports a backdrop of snow-topped mountains and has some amazing over-the-top yachts as well as part of the Italian military fleet. The La Spezia crowd was out with the sunshine, drifting up and down the quais, admiring the boats. Dinner tonight was mediocre chicken followed by the short ride home.

Monday, 2/16/15 Train to Aulla to continue the walk; walked to Villafranca (Stayed in Pontremoli)

Back to reality today. I said Goodbye to Sylvia and Riomaggiore and trained back to Aulla to continue walking. It was a cool gray day to walk the 15k up to Villafranca.

Tuesday, 2/17/15 Villafranca to Pontremoli

I think I'm lucking into a week of beautiful spring sunshine for my climb up into higher country. This morning at Villafranca was the kind of day that just makes you want to walk. My first turn in the road led me up to Borgo Filetto, where I found sitting beside the trail a contented, sleepy golden retreiver. He was sitting at the edge of his elevated front yard, overlooking the sidewalk, with his paws hanging over the edge of the yard, waiting for any and all who walked by to reach up and give him a scratch. I obliged, he thanked me, then he got ready for the next guy who was walking up as I left.

The trail today was wet and green, much of it muddy, but a beautiful walk. It led me to Pontremoli, a town at the junction of rivers that features a beautiful gray castle nove the centro storico. The castle now houses a museum of menhirs, stone carvings that range in age from1500 to 2500 years old. The area is famous for the concentration of these stones that have been uncovered here.

I indulged in a big dinner tonight--pasta with mushrooms followed by stewed rabbit with salad. I'm fueling up for my climb tomorrow over the Cisa Pass.

Wednesday 2/18/15.

There has to be a couple of days like this one on every long walk, it seems. I was prepped for a hard day, but not for one this tough.

The route from Pontremoli up to Berceto was listed as 25k. I can walk that distance on pavement, with breaks, in 5 hours. This day, on the hiking path, it took me 10.

The trail marked for Francigena hikers is a winding, rocky path that features a few spectacular climbs to beautiful views. I'm using some decent "primitive" trail maps, but they're created for hikers moving north-to-south. Most of the trail markers are also planted with this in mind. That situation is gradually improving as more of us walk "a contrario ", but there are many times every day when a turn marking is hidden or unclear to someone walking northward. That situation was worsened today as part of the trail itself (including trail markers) was obscured by knee-deep snow. That's my long-winded rationalization for losing the trail several times and having to backtrack to reclaim it.

The first part of the climb was hard, and I didn't like early on seeing a cross beside the trail...like a memorial to some old guy who died trying to climb the fool hill. Then I saw three more crosses and realized they were a stations-of-the-cross kind of thing. Which, when I thought about it, was also not too comforting.

I was starting to notice how slow my progress was and

trying to make up some time when I came to a river crossing and found the bridge washed out, the remnants of the cable crossing thrown up on the bank of the opposite shore. I tried to work up and down the bank, looking for a dry way to cross, but the briars and brush were too thick to bushwhack through. I finally gave up, pressed for time, and decided to wade it. This meant having to wrap some gear (phone, camera, etc) in drysacks in case I got dunked, which seemed pretty likely. The river wasn't that wide, but it was fast and snow runoff...very cold. Sure enough, The current did decide to give me one quick butt-dunk, but no gear damage. I just got to climb up into the snow with wet britches. (I don't know how Jeremiah Johnson or The Revenant did it!) This wasn't the only time I lost on the trail today.

The toughest one of those losses was after 7 hours of almost constant climbing. I topped a ridge and had convinced myself it was time to descend. Both the descending trail and a tiny path that cut back up the hill over my shoulder were buried in snow. I didn't even see the uphill route as a real path, and no markers were in sight. I headed downhill, tromping through the snow, grateful to be headed down instead of up for a change. After a couple of hundred yards of this, a sharp descent, I realized that I still wasn't seeing trail marks and that I'd missed a turn. I hate to backtrack. I especially hate to backtrack back up a hill I just climbed. In this case, it looked to me like I could bushwhack my way straight up the side of the mountain to where the "up" trail must be.

There are bits of animal trails here and there that convince me I can do this, even with a heavy pack. And it turns out that I could do it, but on hands and feet and knees, scrabbling for every little weed and scrub for balance. What's a little embarrassing is that all over the side of this mountain are small stacks of cut wood that someone has harvested and stacked to pick up later. I'm barely surviving my way up the hill where someone has been able to use a chainsaw and spend days stacking cordwood.

At the crest of the hill (finally), huffing like a rented mule, I found a trail and remnants of an old trail marker that convinced me I was back on track. The "trail" was still under snow, but I could find a good prospect for one. I headed on up. The patchy snow changed to a solid snow cap, so I rolled down my pants legs, pulled on my gaiters, and strapped a pair of YakTrax to the bottom of my boots. I'm slogging down what I think is a trail, wondering if I'm off track, when I hear a clanking ahead. I found a corner and see a lineman up a ladder on a telephone relay tower, up in the wind, slaving away in the cold. I see his tracks in the snow and follow them another half k to where he had to park his truck and trek up to the tower.

Shortly after, I hit pavement at last and could walk the road on up to the Passo Della Cisa. Was surprised to find an open bar/cafe at the top. I would love to have sat and warmed up, but dusk had caught me, and I had another 9k to go before I could find a bed. The north side of the mountain was deep in snow, but the road was clear and traffic non-existent. I stumbled (literally) into Berceto an hour after dark and lucked into a little B&B (Casa dei Noni) with real hot water and was saved. The one ristorante open in town on a Wednesday night had a roaring fire and solid food, a combination that can quickly erase the pain of a hard climb.

I think I'll sleep in tomorrow.

Thursday, 2/19/15

Day off to recover in Berceto. Sleep is a good thing. Heat and hot water are amazing luxuries.

Friday, 2/20/15
UNDER THE EMILIA-ROMAGNA SUN, or
IT'S A SMALL CONTINENT

A few years ago when I conducted the Chamber Singers I took them on a concert tour through parts of Switzerland and Italy. There were lots of memorable moments during the adventure--performing in St. Mark's among them. One of the most fun was one of those small-world moments that can't be planned.

In searching for concert venues for the group, I found we were able to book a tiny little church near the Rialto Bridge that claimed to be the oldest church in the city. It was a wonderful space for us--small, intimate, historic, and with large doors we could open to the street to let our music welcome passersby into the concert. We had handed out flyers announcing the event during the day, but as expected, the crowd at the beginning of the concert was small. No matter...we'd sung to tiny crowds before.

By the end of the concert the house was full, and the response of the crowd was enthusiastic. We were mingling and thanking the audience after the event when a lady stopped me to ask in her sweetest Southern alto, "Now, where are y'all from?!" When I told her where the college is, she brightened and told me she happened to know my Dean through a college connection.

Just a year later I was walking through Lucca when I saw a familiar face. Jan Gosnell, one of our adjunct art faculty at the college, was walking out of a cafe with a group from Fayetteville on a group tour with KUAF, our local public radio station.

Yesterday's encounter seemed even more random and interesting to me. I was walking out of Berceto, up and over the mountain behind the city, trying to decide whether to stop at Cassio, a little hillside town 2k up the road. It was a clear, cold morning, but the sun was at my back, highlighting the snow fields across the valley to the east. I was passing a large house with a young couple in the front yard, he on the phone and she petting a lazy yellow dog. I noticed a small pilgrim symbol on her front door just as she waved to me and signaled to invite me to stop for a coffee.

That's when I noticed the guy on the phone, smoking and talking and waving at me. I stopped and stared...you just don't really expect to bump into people you know on a quiet mountain road in the Italian outback. He was still deep into his conversation, but I asked the girl if that was Federico, and she confirmed it, obviously wondering how I knew.

Back in the summer of 2012 I'd spent time in the north of the country, trying to improve my Italian grammar and then walking for a few weeks up near the

Swiss border. I was spending a few days here and there on the Via Francigena, trying out the trail, wondering if it was a pilgrimage that I wanted to dedicate a few months to trying. I saw few other pilgrims on that trip. Unlike the Spanish pilgrimage, El Camino de Santiago, this one might draw many day-hikers and week-hikers like me, but few who tackle the entire 1100-mile route between London and Rome.

One of the half-dozen others I walked with was a young guy who worked in a libreria, bookstore in Parma. He was good company and had enough English to help me over the language gaps. We walked through some farmlands and rice fields together, swatted at clouds of mosquitoes, and then went our separate ways. A week later, on the last night of his walk that summer, we happened to end up in the same hostel in Pontremoli.

The hostel there is in a 16th Century castle that stands guard from a perch on the north side of the city. It's one of the most interesting hostels I've seen on the route in that the castle is also a museum of stelle, primitive stone sculptures unearthed in the region. Pilgrims are welcomed to the hostel with--literally--the keys to the castle. We're asked to lock the door behind us if we leave for dinner.

Federico had picked up a small family of unattached hikers, but their group was splitting up at Pontremoli, all heading in different directions. I went out for an early dinner, and as I came back into the castle, I heard eerie moans coming from the walls. I thought maybe the ghosts of pilgrims past were walking the walls that night. Sure enough, as I rounded a corner to an interior courtyard, I saw two figures in white floating down a staircase...and Federico standing below, filming them on his iPhone. I later found out that the last-night celebration of the group had involved a couple of bottles of vino rosso. With that information, the impromptu cinematic effort made perfect sense.

I said goodbye to Federico the next morning, not expecting to see him again. It's the nature of these pilgrimage trails, though, to defy odds in personal connections. When I bumped into him again today, it seemed amazing, but yet, in the context of the trail, believable.

His partner, Rosanna, welcomed me into the house where we shed our boots at the door and settled in for a coffee in the kitchen. A noisy group of brothers, sisters, girl-and-boyfriends trooped through the space, introducing themselves (Andrea, Guillermo, Paola, Davide/Bau, Carlo, and the two dogs, Lana and Reggy) and grabbing snacks off the table.

Federico finished his business call and joined us, giving me a hug and baci and laughing at the improbability of the situation. He still works in another city but just happened to be on holiday this week, working at home. He just happened to have stepped outside just now for a smoke and the phone call when I just happened to be walking down the road. I wasn't going to stop, but Rosanna happened to have invited me for coffee and caught my attention...etc., etc.

It's fascinating to me when divergent lives cross on the road. When I walked with Federico in 2012, we found that both of us had walked the Spanish Camino and were searching for a similar experience here. He told me that one of his dreams was to find a house he could open as a hostel for pilgrims.

Two and a half years later, Federico has a firm hold on that dream. The house he found soon after that summer is a huge old farmstead on a little more than 3 hectares (around 8 acres) of land. The home was started in 1890 and therefore had some expected as well as unexpected challenges. The 2-foot-thick walls gave him a firm structure but make any alterations to the layout challenging. He and Rosanna and his gang of friends/family have already made habitable a couple of bedrooms, bathrooms, living room, kitchen, and a large attic for pilgrim bunks. They've rebuilt a barn for their own rough storage and a "party room" that they lit with candles and filled with music for their move-in celebration. There is still another barn that was used for hay storage that is waiting in line for work, and the part of the house that is not yet livable is larger than the part in use now.

Their latest project idea was to finish the large basement room beneath the kitchen, thinking that it would make another warm winter living space. Federico was on the phone this morning with a plumber after they discovered that their kitchen water was draining down into the ground below the kitchen. The room they'd started excavating was filling with the leaking water. He said this was pretty typical of every part of the work so far--every bit of planned work leads to surprises that extend the job. He was smiling and happy as he said it, though, obviously enjoying the challenge. It's already a great space and promises to be filled with happy pilgrims in the future.

I needed to walk, and Federico needed to plumb, so we swapped hugs again and said goodbye. Rosanna laughed again about the unlikely meeting,, but Federico just shook his head. "It's the Camino," he said.

****

My head was spinning for the rest of the day. Fortunately, it's an easy slide down the mountain with no traffic. Just above Fornovo di Taro, the road passes an interesting volcanic rock formation that rises from the hillside, startlingly different from its surroundings. The Italians have set it aside as a natural preserve and made large parts of it accessible to everyone, including physically challenged.

Saturday, 2/21/15

Found a nice little albergo over an Irish Pub last night. I'm in Fornovo to cross the Taro River and continue. Drizzly, gray, cold.

Sunday, 2/22/15

Best of intentions to get up and walk today, regardless of the weather. Made the mistake first thing this morning of checking the forecast on TV--39F and raining. Decided to make this a resting/writing day instead of a soaking-wet-walking day.

No morning heat in my room today, so I headed to a cafe in the center of Fidenza. Via Cavour--the Italian equivalent of JFK or MLK Blvd--is blocked to traffic. The Piazza Giuseppe Garibaldi is decorated with race banners and a large inflatable finish line. Organizers for this year's marathon drew a miserable weather day, but they still drew a great mob of runners willing to fight the rain. I felt a little guilty...but then my cappuccino came, and I got over it.

I've had a comfortable two nights in the same Hotel Ariston, the place built over an Irish Pub. Their "pub food" is a step above most of the meals I've eaten on the road. Thursday night I went for a hamburger and got something that tasted like...well, like a real hamburger. Pretty amazing outside the U.S. to get a good ole 'Merican burger. Just before it arrived at my table, an older man came in and was talking to the manager. He looked at me, asked me if I understood Italian, then walked on over and invited himself to sit down. Tullio, ("the same as one of our emperors") is a friendly guy who just wanted to chat.

He's the patriarch of the family that owns the hotel and pub. He was concierge at large hotels in France, Germany, and Switzerland during his career, but he said, "Now, I'm 75. I'm tired." But then he got re-energized telling tales of a few famous guests he took care of, including the last Shah of Iran and James Stewart. According to Tullio, Stewart showed up at his hotel in Torino driving a pink Cadilac.

About this time my burger arrived, and Tullio's daughter, Cinzia, shooed him away from my table so he could eat. Did I mention that it was a really good burger?

The next day after a day of walking around the city, I worked my way back to the pub for dinner again. I was just about to have a look at the menu to convince myself to try something besides the burger when Simone, Tullio's son, came out of the kitchen. He waved a dish of pasta at me. "Have you tried this?, he asked. "It's crespelle alla parmigiana, and Tullio just made it for us. You should try it!" I did...and was glad of it.

The dish is similar to a stuffed manicotti, but with smaller pillows of pasta. His version was filled with ricotta and prosciutto crudo, but Simone told me it's sometimes filled with spinach as well.

Today, after an easy day over coffee, I had an early dinner of bacon and eggs in a local cafe. I stopped into the pub for an after-dinner amaro and bumped into Tullio. I complimented him on the crespelle, and ten minutes later he was at my table waving a pan of freshly made lasagne under my nose. I protested, explained that I ate early tonight. He wanted to know if I'd ever eaten lasagne before, and of course I assured him I had. He said, "In Parma? In this region?" I confessed that it wasn't here. "Then you haven't had real lasagne. This is the best!"

He went back to he kitchen, and I went back to my book. Ten minutes later he was back at my table with a sample, insisting that I taste it. "I want to make sure you've had real lasagne."

He was right again--it's delicious...less tomato than its American cousin, but strong on ricotta and herbs. He told me that it's the homemade pasta that makes a big difference, too. "Nothing from a big company, but from my kitchen."

Each night his family drifted by in groups, keeping the table nearest the kitchen busy with kids and grandkids, everybody stopping for a plate of whatever Tullio was in the mood to bring in that night. The crowd--most known to the family--drifted through, the soccer game was always on the big screen in the corner, and the aroma of pasta, red wine, and Guinness filled the room.

Last night was karaoke, starting just before midnight. I fell asleep to the thump of Italian love songs and old American pop. Tonight is Latin Night, so I guess I'll have salsa dreams to go with memories of Tullio's lasagne.

*******. Postscript

As I was getting ready to leave, Tullio drifted by again to say goodbye. He grabbed my empty amaro glass and before I could protest, he filled it again. "Piccola", he said. "Just a little." He asked where I was headed next, and I listed the towns up the trail. "Send me a card...maybe I answer." He left, and Cinzia said the drinks were on the house.

They're running two hotels and trying to sell this one, but I hope it's still here the next time I'm in town.

A SPOT OF TROUBLE

I lay in bed this morning at the Hotel Serena and thought of just rolling over and staying the day in town. Probably should have.

But, Iva, the owner, assured me that the day would be beautiful, fresca...cooler than yesterday. He gave me (too fast to follow) a list of the amazing sights I'd get to see. Finally, he pointed me to the first steps of that day's trail...not along the flat road, but up into the mountains again.

You'd think I'd learn, but I don't. The farther away I get from the flat valley road the more trouble I find. Yes, that flat road has traffic to deal with, but the alternative trail up and down the mountains is just that--up and down mountains. Mostly up, as far as I could tell.

Today's trail promised to show me a medieval castle built by the Montjovet family, and sure enough, within an hour's walk, I could part the branches on the bushes and see the citadel perched on the mountain ahead. It's a great gray fortress, complete with crenolated walls, turrets and towers...everything you'd want in your community castle.

It was at this point that the grassy path split, one side heading downhill, and the other decidedly up. The sign for hikers (most of these trails have occasional signs) had fallen over and was lying beside the trail. It was anyone's guess which was correct, but if given a choice, I'll generally think "downhill". Bad choice #2.

After a half mile of slogging through weeds, the path started dwindling, the weeds started winning...and then won. I came to a cliff and could look down on top of the town, but it was straight down--200 feet below me. I hate backtracking, especially when it's uphill, so--bad choice#3--I looked up. I thought that surely (!) there must be another trail somewhere nearby that would lead me to civilization. It couldn't be below me, so it had to be above.

I started scrabbling on hands and knees up the side of the mountain, aiming for an old terrace above me. Terraces are man-made, right? Someone had to be able to walk in and out to build them, right? Yes, had to be so, but these terraces were hundreds of years old, and any trails to them were long gone. After a half hour of uphill guesswork, I looked up, and...there was Montjovet Castle, 200 feet directly above me.

My first thought was relief--I'd be able to find a road down from the castle. After looking around for a way up, however, reality hit. The reason they built these old fortresses on a rocky point was so that the bad guys couldn't climb up the mountain and surprise you. I prowled around (hands and knees still) in every direction and could see no way up.

This wasn't a hill, understand. It was a real mountain. A by-god Alp. Really a great choice to get stuck on, right?

I have rock climbing friends that could do this rock. There are some obvious handholds, a few seemingly-easy bits...but with no ropes or backup, and with my heavy pack, I knew I was out of my league. I was frustrated not only that I couldn't go farther up, but

I knew I'd have trouble going back down the way I'd come. Nothing for it but to try, though.

I had a moment, sitting there trying to get my breath back and my heart-rate down, when I realized that this is how hikers get stuck on the side of a mountain and have to call for a rescue squad to come get them. I was fortunate that I wasn't yet exhausted, that the weather was nice, and that I had hours of daylight left. I confess, though, that I thought of the little flip-phone in my pack, wondered if I had enough minutes left on it to do any good or whether if I could reach someone I would be able in my bad Italian to give them close enough directions to reach me.

That choice would come later, though. I still had time and energy to try to get myself down. I started down and as expected, couldn't find the tail end of that "trail" that had led me here. I was doing some serious (not smart, but serious) bushwhacking, butt-sliding, more scrabbling, through thick undergrowth with lots briars and thorns. (Even Italian ones aren't exotic enough to be any fun.)

I'd find my way back to a terrace, think I was on the right level, but then would dead-end into a wall of thorns. Then I'd have to figure out if I was on a higher terrace or had somehow made my way down too low, below the level I needed. Usually I can laugh my way through my misadventures, but this one worried me. It was tiring to move even a little distance in that thick brush while trying to balance on the slopes. My rest stops came more frequently, and the little water left in my bottle was tasting way too good.

One of those rest stops was on the lip of a terrace, and as I sat I saw built into the wall below three steps--familiar ones that I'd crawled up the first time.

Three or four more tries, and I'd found it--the way back...and then lost it...and found it again. I trudged on, gladly backtracking at this point, and could finally laugh a little, then, since I looked like I'd gone right through the front windshield...scratched and bleeding, britches ripped, muddy, twigs and grass and branches stuck all over me. Probably looked like an Italian Bigfoot.

I found the downed sign again and this time took the "hard" road, the high one, up and up to a small village. Fortunately, almost every one of the mountain towns around here has a great public watering hole, a stone or concrete trough with a constant-flowing cool stream of water. As I finally reached the little village of St. Germain, sweaty, dirty, breathing like a tired old jackass (and feeling more than a little like one), I was ready for that cool mountain water. I drank my fill, washed some of the grime and blood, and shook myself like a wet dog. (I know, that's two animals in one paragraph.)

The rest of the day--what was left of it--was downhill from there. Literally. Some of it even in the shade, too. As I wandered on down into the next town, a guy about my age walked up and asked me if I was walking the Via Francigena. He was interested in the walk and wanted to try it someday. Then he commenced to offer me advice on what to see in the area...and everything he pointed to was uphill. Just when you think you've met a nice local citizen, he tries to talk you into climbing a mountain.

JOURNAL, WEEK 7-8

Monday, 2/23/15--Fiorenzuola di Ardia

Unlike drippy yesterday, today is a beautiful, sunny, cold day...perfect for walking...at least for walking a kilometer to a cafe where I can get my breakfast. I loved the little hotel/pub where I stayed the past couple of nights, but their colazione in the morning was as bad as their dinner was good. It consisted of a basket of packaged croissants--actually just a useless roll of white bread disguised as one--and free access to a coin-op coffee machine that put out undrinkable coffee. Well worth skipping. I was happy to stop at a cafe along the route and was lured in by one sporting a life-sized sculpture of Marilyn Monroe in her famous blowing-skirt pose.

The route to Fiorenzuola D'Arda was mostly beside the arrow-straight highway, but occasionally I could find a little parallel country lane to use instead. 7k up the road in Alseno I pulled into another little cafe to rest and happened to invade the local morning coffee klatsch. When I walked in, the half-dozen assorted seniors all froze mid-sentence to stare at the guy with the big backpack, smelling like miles of dirt road and old boots. I gave the password, though---"Buongiorno!"-- and that broke the trance. They immediately wanted to know who I was, where I was going, ("Tutte a piedi?!"), where I started that day, and where I would stop tonight. I got 6 quick opinions on the wisdom or lack of it about this plan, and just like that, they were done with me. I sat down with my coffee, and they returned to politics, the financial crisis in Italy, and local gossip. On the way out the door, though, each wished me luck or a buonagiornata.

Didn't find an easy place to stay in Fiorenzuola, so I got a train 10 minutes up the road to Piacenza. Will return to F early Wednesday to continue the walking.

I did find entertainment of sorts in the big city. Three cinemas were lined up down Emaunele II near my little affitacamere, so I decided to drop in for a showing late that night of 50 Shades of Gray, or Cinquanta Sfumatori di Grigio, as we say on The Continent. It was funny seeing it with this crowd, as they talked and laughed all the way through the show. I dozed through part but made it to the end. I don't think my deficient Italian hurt me much on this one. Glad I only paid $5.

Tuesday 2/24/15--Rain day.

I was glad I had planned to spend this one on a break. I grabbed an early train to Bologna to see my friends Carla and Francesco.

I had met Carla and her friend Francesca a decade earlier in Spain. One night at a dinner of mixed pilgrims in Astorga the three of us struck up a friendship and ended up in company along the trail for the last couple of weeks into Santiago. Carla had joined my Chamber Singers in Rome in 2006 to have fun with us there, and I had met Francesco, a fellow musician, on another stop in Bologna.

The rain followed me to Bologna, but I found a warm welcome there and some great pizza at a friend's ristorante in the city. After a few weeks in hostels and hotels, it was great to share food and hugs with friends.

Wednesday 2/25/15--Piacenza

Thursday, 2/26/15. Piacenza to Castel San Giovanni

This week I've been walking through the Italian region of Emilia-Romagna unknowingly passing only 20k or so from the birthplace of Giuseppe Verdi at Busseto. I should have known I was close as every town I pass seems to have a Via Giuseppe Verdi or a Piazza Verdi. Tonight I'm in the town of Castel San Giovanni. Out searching for dinner, I wandered through a central square, and there I found the Teatro Verdi along with a plaque honoring this composer who is considered by many to be the greatest composer of opera in the 19th Century. [Note to my NWACC friends: currently playing is the Italian version of the play NWACC Theatre produced last fall--Shakespeare a 90 Minuti.]

Verdi's family ran a small ristorante in Busseto, and Verdi started his musical career studying with the church organist in the little town. He practiced his music on a little spinet piano given to his family. I have to imagine that no one in the village imagined that the child playing that little instrument might grow to make such a difference in the world of music. During one three-year period, 1851-1853, he composed three of his most popular operas--Rigoletto, Il Trovatore, and La Traviata.

WALKING WITH A SORE FOOT--A Day Off in Pavia

Two weeks walking now, and I'd forgotten about a problem I usually have with my right foot. It's sore again, in a way that it goes sore on all my long walks. There's a blister right in the middle of the ball of that foot, but it's under a callous...too deep for me to lance. My pinkie has also been squashed enough over the past 150 miles to be aching, too.

So, every time I take a step for the 5-7 hours each day of walking, I register a little pain from that foot.

I'm not pretending this is a huge deal. It's not. It's not crippling, it's not dangerous, it's just...there. All day, every time I step on that foot, it hurts. "Sore" is the word that keeps coming to mind.

I could probably avoid developing this problem if I could make myself slow down at the beginning of a cross-country walk, do shorter days and take more cool-down breaks. Apparently, I'm not able to do this. I get excited about being in a new place, seeing new country or returning to spaces I love. I don't want to stop walking early in the day, or occasionally I can't find a place to stop for the night...and before I know it I've overwalked that foot. A day or two later, a blister blooms..

After the first five minutes of walking on it, the pain moves to a different place in my head, and I forget about the foot for awhile. It's interesting how a regular irritation like that can be forgotten for long periods of time.

It's like this guy I used to know at work who was a major pain in a different part of my body. He's unqualified, inexperienced in our field, but knows how to work the system for promotion. He's blatantly ambitious and self-serving, and those qualities have worked well for him. When he worked with us, it was painful to watch him use the place for his own ambition. However, it was pointless and distracting to spend energy worrying about him. You had to put those thoughts in another part of your brain and just get on with the work.

I think about this with people who suffer real pain--constant, pervasive, serious pain. People show amazing ability to refocus their concentration on something else so that they can get on with their lives.

Distraction helps. Two days ago I limped into the Borgo Ticino on the edge of the great old Medieval city of Pavia. A fairly modern but still impressive covered bridge leads into the city. I cooled for a few minutes in its shade before hobbling around town--and it's a pretty big town--making the rounds of alberghi, looking for a room and having no luck. I hadn't even thought of this possibility, just assuming that the city was big enough that there had to be a room.

No such luck. No room at the hotels, alberghi, affita camere, the local ostello--niente. I had hoped to find a cheap place and take a day off, too, to have a look around the historic place and rest my foot a bit. I borrowed a phone, called around, and found a place to stay in a little albergo 16k up the road. Too far to walk, I decided to take a train, then return the next day to continue the walk.

Albergo della Pesa is a ristorante/hotel in Belgioioso, a town that is as nice as its name sounds. My "train" was actually a bus run by Trenitalia to the areas that just aren't busy enough to need real rail service. I found my way there, checked in, did my ritual shower/laundry-in-the-sink routine, and collapsed for a bit. Amazing, how getting the weight off of a sore hoof helps the pain go away.

The next morning, I left my heavy old backpack in the room and took the train (a real one this time) for the 20 minute ride back to Pavia. Only 20 minutes of comfort on a train, but it would take me three hours plus a break to walk that far.

Pavia on a Saturday June morning is a buzzing place. The station was cluttered out front with bus pickups, idling taxis, the rattle of rolling luggage, and the songs of a few homeless guys sipping from paper bagged bottles and preaching their view of the world. I headed down the Via dal Independenze to the river.

Walking up on the covered bridge from a different angle, I was reminded that I wasn't noticing my foot today. Just getting the weight of the pack off it was helping. Plus, having a day off of serious walking made an immense difference. I sat with the lollers in the portici of the bridge, watching the boaters practice their standing version of rowing for the next day's palio--boat races up and down the river Ticino.

Walking up to the Piazza del Duomo, I found the Saturday market in full swing around the crumbling old church. The building was begun around 1500, and parts of it were in need again of refurbishing. Still, it's a stately, impressive brick structure that seems a bit too dignified to be surrounded by tents and trailers loaded with candies, sausage, roast chickens, cheap sunglasses, jogging shoes made in China and formaggio made down the street.

The shoppers were out, though, enjoying the nice weather and apparently oblivious to any thought of the great old building rising above the river of stalls and umbrellas. Maybe that's another awareness, that, like the pain of a sore foot, gets pushed aside when it is not useful. Whatever becomes common to us fades from our consciousness into a side alley of memory.

The market crowd was enhanced today by a club of medieval re-enactors in full knights' gear, waving swords and clanging armor in a celebration of the city's history. I wandered through the melee' and up through the university at Leonardo da Vinci piazza. Three towers guard the east entrance to the school, and one is showing its age like the duomo. Many of the corners of the 200-foot tower are braced with steel brackets that are trying to prevent the spread of old age that effects the towers in the same way it affects my waistline. The old bricks are decaying like teeth going bad, and...OK, that's one too many anatomical comparisons, but you get the idea. Repairs are in order for body and buildings.

Buildings of the university are like so many other structures in the city--tall but rather plain outside walls, but inside those walls a series of impressive courtyards, ringed with covered walkways, all featuring busts and statues of former faculty and founders. There is a weight to the history here, and I wonder if that translates to the students. Perhaps it, too is like the pain in a foot or the "normal" sight of a 500-year-old cathedral.

A telling sight is the bulletin board hung beneath a couple of those impressive statues. It's jammed with bits of papers, announcements, event posters, want ads, class announcements, plans for protests, graffiti, ads for roommates...a sight that is probably found on university campuses all over the world.

North of the university is a beautiful park surrounding the 17th Century castle. The beautiful old red brick-and-stone fortress, moat now filled with grass and flowers, surrounds a broad courtyard a hundred meters across that is now he site of outdoor concerts. Two levels of covered loggia ring this courtyard, and the building houses a wonderful archeological and cultural/art museum.

Today there is also a gathering of agencies promoting pilgrim trails around the country and Europe, celebrating the continent's history of wanderers and seekers. A photo contest from pilgrims themselves is on display, showing scenes of many of the places I've walked myself.

Even without the pack, walking another 10k around the cobblestone streets is wearing, and I finally chuck it in and head for my room. My day of strolling, just having a look at a city like a tourist would rather than trying to "make miles" with a backpack, has helped heal a bit of that soreness. Tomorrow I'll get a train (bus?) back to Pavia once again to continue the walk toward the next river (the Po) and the next city (Piacenza). I'll do it on a fresh foot, though, and with a lighter step. Sometimes all it takes to help a sore foot is a day away from the source of the pain.

Friday, 2/27/15
Castel San Giovanni to Pavia

Saturday, 2/28/15. Last day of February!

My friend Carla had told me that Certosa di Pavia was a stunning structure, so I decided to se it before I left the city. It's a 10-minute train ride--about 10k--northeast of the city, in a small town surrounded by farms. The structure is indeed impressive, a walled enclosure around perhaps the most ornate and well-preserved monastery in Italy.

The building was begun at the end of the 14th Century on the orders of a Duke Viconti of Milano. An unusually detailed white marble facade rife with intricately-carved figures and polychrome decorations was added to the original red brick structure in the 15th-16th Centuries. The interior is likewise heavily decorated, with multiple ceiling and wall motifs.

The main cloister features 123 marble arches to the courtyard and 24 independent and distinctive cell-homes as habitation for the monks.

Sunday, 3/1/15

Pavia to Garlasco --Another generally quiet Sunday walk through agricultural fields northwest of Pavia. Walked through Gropello Cairolli where a stranger in the bar asked all about the pilgrimage, then warned me about leaving my backpack exposed in the bar. On the way out of that town, I bumped into another pellegrino, only the second I've met on the trail. Fiedrich is German, from a small town near Dortmund. He's been doing the trail from his home toward Rome in two-week stretches. Just a few more and he'll be there. I was reminded of a group of my friends in the Fayetteville Meet-up hiking group who have conquered the Ozark

Highlands Trail in similar fashion, taking it a few days at a time over the course of a few months. It's a different experience than a straight-through hike, but both methods have their advantages and challenges.

Monday, 3/2/15. Texas Independence Day. (1836--Texas declares The Republic)

Garlasco to Mortara--Today was a day of rice fields, irrigation canals, and another pilgrim. Lots of grays and browns in the landscape now, but I could taste a little spring in the air. Walked through Tromello on the road and then turned onto a trail through an agri area. As I passed a large farm holding, I spied another walker in the distance. His head was down and there was a bit of a limp in his gait. When we were close, he looked up, a bit startled by another walker. His backpack gave him away as a pilgrim, but he was too clean and fresh to have been long on the road.

His name was Roberto, and yes, he'd just been walking a few days. He had started in the Val D'Aosta and was hoping to walk to Rome. "Ma, e dificile!", he confessed. I got the feeling he might reconsider and head home to train more before trying the whole route. He's right--it is difficult.

One of the difficult parts is the relentless nature of the long-distance walk. It's hard enough to put in the miles for a day or two or ten, but no matter how interesting the scenery or how great the weather, body and mind start to rebel after weeks of the routine.

Tuesday, 3/3/15

Mortara to Palestro (Vercelli)

Hit one of those days when I couldn't buy a Francigena trail marker. It wasn't a huge problem, but it's a bit annoying. In this region the markers are less prevalent than in others, and they're almost all oriented to someone walking north-to-south. It can be surprisingly hard --and irritating--to search for them against the grain.

Today, after just a few k, I promptly lost the markers coming out of Madonna Del Campo. The land was flat, and the day was clear, so it wasn't a question of being lost, but rather one of how to get to Nicorvo, visible 6k ahead, without stumbling into an irrigation canal or walking through someone's private patch and having my backside chewed by a farm dog.

I'm happy to tell you that the locals aren't as rabid about private property as we in the South/Southwest of the US are. I was wandering all over freshly plowed rice fields, looking for raised dikes to get me out of the mud.

These fields haven't been planted yet, or I'd have had trouble getting through them. The rice farmers are busy shaping their fields and irrigation systems, trimming brush out of the canals, and turning fertilizer into the land. "Aromatic" would be one way to think of today's route.

I found my way through the mud and was ready for a coffee at Nicorvo, one of the small villages on the historic route. As I spied the only bar, though, I was waved to the curb by an elderly couple in a passing car. The driver asked me if I was really a pellegrino, then climbed out of the car with a big smile, ready to hug me. (They stopped in the middle of the street, but didn't seem worried about traffic flow in Nicorvo.). They were just happy to spot their first pilgrim of the season and wanted to let me know that he had written a book about this part of the trail. He promised to send me a copy, handed me a candy for the walk, then drove away.

The bar was a hundred yards up the street and calling my name. Just inside the door was the security guard, a sleepy white Scottie. He managed to lift his head for a scratch before rolling over on his door mat and resuming his duty. The manager of the bar was ready to celebrate the first pilgrim-spotting, too, and gave me my cappuccino for free. She said it would bring her luck for the year. I was happy to be of service.

I arrived in Robbio early, had a focaccia and a coke, then looked for a bed.

A LITTLE GNOME
Bell Dreams in Robbio

There's a small bell tower in the Italian town of Robbio, and it chimes on the quarter hour. Light, high pitched, on the dainty side, the bells lend a flavor to the town that I can imagine the local citizens have come to enjoy.

And then there's the larger tower just outside my window. I'm in a room of the hostel run by the local police. The giant bells there are timed to ring 20" after those other bells. Remember? The lighter, dainty ones? These are different. Heavy, clanky, low pitched, and loud...these sound like they were molded from a few dead Humvees.

I just got up from a long nap that was punctuated by this War of the Bells drifting in and out and all over my weird dreams. It appears that I'll be treated to this concert all night tonight on the quarter hours. This is one of the delights of the walking life that I forget about when I'm back home dreaming of another long walk and nights in "basic" hostels.

This night will be coming off the worst night of the walk so far. For the past day or two I've been off my feed, feeling lightheaded and more tired than I should. Not sure if I got some bad water or just a stomach bug of some kind, but last night it all came to a "head". Was up all night running to the WC down the hall, paying for my sins.

The last thing I wanted to do was get up this morning, put on that heavy pack, and walk in the sun for six hours. But, the little overpriced grubby hotel where I had a room wasn't available for another night, I couldn't find another hotel in the town, so there was nothing for it but to walk.

Out on the edge of town I was shuffling along like an invalid, and a little local guy with a day pack caught up with me. I was standing at a crossroads, trying to figure out which was the shortest route, and GiGi (Pierluigi) Serrata, a retired postal inspector, took over the decision. He was walking the same direction as me and insisted that we walk "by the river".

I could smell "longer" and "harder on the feet" written all over that advice, but I didn't have the strength to argue. Besides, GiGi was a local guy who was dying to show off the nice little trail he's walked so many times. He's guiding a group of 20 young hikers on this road next week, and he just wanted to make sure he remembered it.

He's 76. I mention this because he walked me into the ground. I must have looked like crap, because he kept asking me if I needed to stop and rest.

And I did need to, but of course, I couldn't let a man 16 years older than me show me up so badly. It didn't help that the road was gravel (hard on the feet), not a stitch of shade in sight, and nowhere near the river.

We did walk beside rice paddies and irrigation canals all morning, but I'm not sure that counts as a "river". After 3 hours of shuffling through the gravel, we did come within 100 yards of the Fiume Sestra, close enough to get a glimpse, but not really "beside the river".

Regardless, we finally made it to town, and I found a shady tree to stretch out under for a nap. GiGi gave me the two-cheek kiss, wished me buona giornata, and headed for the typical local huge lunch. After lunch, he would walk back the same trail, while I slogged on another hour to Robbio. My stomach had settled, but my head was in a different time zone. I'd cultivated a new limp, and one foot felt bruised from the gravel.

An hour later I stumbled into the Piazza della Liberta' but couldn't find the address listed for the community's hostel. The men at the bar/cafe' on the corner pointed me toward the police. I looked confused, I guess, because the loudest of the men, a little gnome of a guy who seemed to be performing for the group walked across the street to show me the door. I thanked him, and he gave me a big smile that showed off all his brown stubs. As he turned away, he must have done a good eye-roll over the ignorant Yank, because all his cronies at the bar had a chuckle. Nothing new there...I'm used to that sound.

A good looking woman in a blue uniform opened the door and almost started laughing at how whipped I look. Uncalled for, I thought. But, she did lead me immediately up a nearby flight of stairs to what passes for the local town's attempt at an hostel for pilgrims in La Via Francigena.

This one has three rooms--one filled with extra mattresses stacked around two single beds, one is a bathroom, and a third room with two sad single cots. And I was happy to be there. I picked one of the single cots, had my shower, washed my shorts, and collapsed on the bed to listen to the bells.

German visions joined the weird bell dreams as I woke an hour later to find two strangers standing in the room. Hank and Eva are from Germany, near the border with Netherlands, and they'd just moved into the room with all the mattresses. She's walked for almost three months from their home in Germany, heading for Rome. Hank drives their van and rolls his eyes when he talks about her walk. I don't have much German, and neither of them speaks English, so I think this will be a hand-signal friendship.

They did help roust me from my musical sleep, though, so I pulled on my pants and headed to the bar for a glass of pear juice. (I'm a hard-drinkin' guy.) These small town bars have their regular clientele, all of whom seem to know each other. I was reading a paperback and listening to them all pick on the teenage son of the owner when my buddy, the Gnome, walked in. He "Ciao'd"everyone and even gave me a wave, then proceeded to entertain this crowd, too. He never sat down, just prowled the room, talking much too loudly for the space and using the word "bastardi" a lot more than he probably needed to.

A good book helps pass slow hours in a strange town, but I still had energy to stroll the place a bit. I turned a corner down an alley and found a small row of strange, beautifully designed houses. I was snapping pictures when the guy from the kebab shop (there seems to be one in every little town) told me to turn the corner for the front view. Sure enough, I was at the back of a 17thCentury castello. I turned another corner and found the old moat and drawbridge still intact. The castle isn't huge, but it's impressive, a treasure hidden behind a modern bank and a grocery store.

After my evening stroll, I headed back toward the hostel, only to find the outer door to the courtyard locked and me with no key. It seems like the same old guys were sitting at the cafe', and they laughed and yelled at me. I turned to look, and they were all pointing at my friend, the Gnome. He was back at this cafe'. He gave a disgusted shake of his head and started cursing at the world in general for sending a helpless pellegrino out among the wolves of the night in such a way. Peppered with "bastardi, bastardi", of course.

He walked across the street and pulled a big key ring out of his pocket, unlocking the gate and slipping inside with me. He wanted to know my story, and I thought about feeding him one so that he'd have something to sell back at the bar. Tiredness won out, though, and I gave him the short version of the truth, figuring that's about all I can handle tonight. We parted friends, and I climbed back up to my little paradise in the bell tower, looking forward to catching up on dreams of Quasimodo.

[Postscript: 6:30am the next morning, I loaded up and walked out early, hoping to beat the heat. The day's road was straight and well-marked. I came to the main intersection of the town, and there, yelling at me from across the street, was the Gnome, this time dressed in the optic orange jumpsuit of a street crew. He saw me looking at a map and gestured me to follow him.

I trailed behind as he led me like Moses leading the Israelites through the foot traffic of early workers. All seemed to know him, calling to him, asking why he wasn't working. He, of course, was responding loudly and importantly ("bastardi, bastardi") that he had to show another pilgrim how to find his way out of town.

He led me a couple of hundred unnecessary yards, past lots of Via Francigena signs, and finally stopped beside the Chiesa di San Pietro to point me in the direction of several more of the same signs. We parted again with a wave, this time for good. I think.]

Wednesday, 3/4/15, to Vercelli

A beautiful, if uneventful walk to Vercelli.

Thurday, 3/5/15. Vercelli to Viverone

I stopped at the front desk of the hotel to check out this morning. The night man was still on duty, finishing a long shift. I wasn't wearing my backpack, and he didn't know I was walking the Francigena trail. I paid, he gave me a receipt, and then with a smile, he gave me a lovely parting gift from the hotel--a bag of rice from a local farm. A five-pound bag of rice. I almost did a spit-take, but held it in. After all, it's a great idea to give every guest a little treat like that from a local producer. Smart. I explained that I was on foot, and he got it...grinned and asked me to sign their pilgrims' log. (I am their first pilgrim-guest of the year.). When I came downstairs ten minutes later, geared up and ready to walk, he stopped me and offered me a different treat--a CD of information about the Vercellese area. "Tutte inglese, et piu ligere," he explained with a smile. He was right--it was light enough to carry. Some people here are just determined to be nice. I like it.

The way is straight and sunny and cold today. The temp is only 45F, but there is a 10-15mph Wind blowing down off the Alps ahead. That snowy breeze is a signal of what's ahead. The mountains are larger and closer today, and I can see the Aosta Valley cutting it's way up through them. I've been walking beside a canal that channels one of the rivers down towards all the rice and corn fields. My target today is beyond Santhia at Viverone, on the edge of the lake of that name.

Friday, 3/6/15. Viverone to Ivrea

The lake was almost too nice to leave behind today. The 3k from Viverone around to the north end where the road turns away went too fast. There was a great little cafe sitting there in a park on the lakeshore, unused, inviting...it seemed like the proper thing to do to stop for a last cappuccino before leaving the lake.

The following 4k to Cavaglia, though, were almost as nice as the road turned well into the valley that splits the Alps all the way up to the St. Bernard Pass. I'm walking in the mountains now, but the rise in elevation up the valley is so slight that there's no awareness of climbing. It's an easy walk (relatively) through interesting towns. The houses are starting to show more of an Alpine style, with a chalet thrown in now and then.

I wanted to walk on past Ivrea, but the city talked me into stopping for the night. The river through the south part of town has been restructured to include a kayaking course, and there was a brave soul working the gates when I walked by. A Rocket Cafe in the center offered a hamburger that was recognizable, so I considered the night a "win".

Saturday, 3/7/15. Ivrea to Bard

What a lucky string of weather days! Sunshine and 36 this morning, and the road is again a path through startlingly white peaks and blue skies. I'll sit for a coffee and to read or write for a minute, and when I look up, I'm stunned all over again.

I was having one of those luckiest-guy-in-the-world mornings when an old guy on a bike pulled up from behind me, close enough to make me jump, and asked if I was walking the Francigena. He had pedaled out of his driveway in Borgofranco D'Ivrea as I walked by and was happy to see a pellegrino, his first spotting of the season. (In another month we'll be as common as crows.).

We talked while we walked, and I found out Leonardo had recently walked from Aosta down to Rome in two legs in separate years. He was still energized about the experience and happy to talk about the trail. He'd also walked the Camino in Spain. He said he'd like to walk with me today...but he had to buy groceries for his wife. As he turned into the parking lot for the Carrefour, he wished me a "Buon camino!" I think he'd rather have been walking than shopping for bananas.

It always gives me a spurt of energy when a stranger connects like that. I know it's not really me that attracts them, but rather the backpack-and-boots package, the image of the pilgrim reminding them of their own walks. Whatever...it feels good when someone stops to talk.

I had just walked off from Leonardo when I saw on the street another display of a little sweet wafer called canestrello. I ducked into the cafe and asked for a sample, and it turned out I was in the perfect spot for a taste--La Bottega del Canestrello. This cafe specialized in all flavors of the thin, crisp sweet wafers. The 3-inch disks are a rich mixture of flavors from red wine, moscato, and rum.

I told the man at the counter I was a pellegrino and was just curious for a taste. He picked an assortment of 4 flavors for me and wouldn't accept any money. That kind of kindness continues to find me along this trail and really makes me glad I've passed this way.

Sunday, 3/8/15. Bard to Saint Vincent

Actually Hone, on the north side of Bard, up to Saint Vincent. I couldn't find a place to stay in Bard, so I trained up to Verres, 6k up the road. Got up before breakfast this morning, trained back to Hone and walked back to Verres to earn my coffee.

It was cold this morning--19F, with a fresh little north breeze in my teeth. But, what a gorgeous day to be walking in the Valle D'Aosta! I've been by Forti di Bard several times before, but it is always impressive to me to see that monstrous structure perched on the hill. Seeing it early in the morning with the sun coming up the valley behind it is a special sight. I can put aside considerations of its purpose and history and enjoy the sight itself.

My early road through the valley was a quiet, cold, Sunday morning walk through vineyards, campgrounds, pens of sheep, smoking chimneys, and a few other guys who drew the short straw and had to walk the dog this morning. A giant old furry German shepherd stood in the middle of the lane and glared at me as I walked into Arnad, and I thought we were going to have to negotiate safe passage. When I got close, though, he kind of gave up the glare and just leaned into me for a scratch. That seemed to do it for the toll this morning, and I was allowed to pass in peace. I sat down at breakfast in Verres with an appetite, and then moved on to Montjovet.

It was here a few years back that I split my britches on the side of the mountain east of the road. The castle of St. Germain--the remains, anyway--have a great vantage point over the valley from high above, stacked on a rocky hilltop. I had approached from the north that time, following the signposts for the Francigena...until I came to the one knocked down and lying by the road. It was at a fork, so I got to choose--up the hill or traverse the side. Being a guy who takes the easy way when he can, I opted for the traverse. Obviously--since there's a story here--it was the wrong way. But, by the time the trail died away on a steep hillside full of high weeds and brambles, I'd walked another half k and didn't want to backtrack. I could see stone terraces above me stepping up the hill toward the fortress walls and thought that, surely if someone could get up there to build those walls, I could bushwhack up a ways and find a way up to the castle. All I found, though, were more briars, steeper climbs, and sharp drops to the rocks below. It was one of those moments of clarity when I knew 1) I could fall and die, and 2) I might not be able to find my way back down to the trail. I did have a little phone for texting with me, but I didn't know who I'd even call to ask for help. Fortunately it didn't come to that. After another half hour of stumbling around in the brush I fell back onto the tail end of that trail and drug myself back to that fallen signpost. (I kicked it on the way by just to teach it a lesson.)

Today's not-great memory happened because I was walking the road this time rather than getting lost up on the hillside. No getting lost for me today, but I did learn that the road gets narrower as it rises into the side of the mountain. There is no real shoulder or place to walk, and the curves are tight with bad sight-lines for drivers. In short, it's not a place for people to walk. Or to ride bikes, for that matter, but climbing the road behind me were the normal teams of local cyclists out for their weekend workout. I drug on into Saint Vincent and found a bunk. A beer and a plate of pasta were all I needed to seal the day.

CUTTING CORNERS, BREAKING RULES
Confessions of an Evangelical Jaywalker

7 June, 2015,
Sunday morning at the Malibu Bar, Ladispoli, Italy
And 8 June, Lago di Bracciano

That's me--rule breaker. Big time lawless individual. You want somebody to show you how to jaywalk, I'm your man. Probably. If the way is clear, that is...no authorities around. Why, I've been known to cross against the light, cross in the middle of a block, step outside the paint on a crosswalk...yessir, it's a dark past, but I'm owning it.

Ahh, it's such a warm feeling I get when I see one ahead of me. After miles walking beside a straight road, I look up, and there it is--a roundabout! That miracle invention by some driver-in-a-hurry that lets us skip a stop sign and pull straight out into moving traffic, 'cause God knows, we don't want to ever slow down if we can help it.

For a walker, it's magic. Cars can't hop the curb and cut through, but I can...walk straight across the road and through the dead middle of that traffic circle. Cut through it like ants in the grass, just walk right across it like it's not there. I'm not saying it's smart or safe, just that it feels good to cut through the middle.

Crosswalks are definitely the safe way to go, but they make me crazy. Clearly they were/are designed by folks who don't walk for a living or else they wouldn't add steps to our day. Here in Italy they at least understand that people will indeed be walking and at some point they will want to cross a road, a fact most American towns ignore. Even here, though, planners start with the idea that cars come first--we can't interrupt the smooth flow of traffic. Walkers can come to a corner and often find it blocked with railings preventing a crossing, funneling us 20, 30, 50 feet away to a railing gap before we find the magic space.

I think in general we're finding too many rules bordering our lives these days, and that we should all be about the business of breaking a few just for good measure.

Recently I saw an article in Bloomberg Business offering yet another restriction. The author's admonition was that we shouldn't be signing off our emails with "Best". I mean, really...is this a rule that somebody needs to see enforced?

Facebook and social media in general want to fill our heads with lists of rules--10 reasons for this, and 19 reasons for that.

One of the nice things --one of the few, actually— about getting older and further along in a career is that you don't have to think so hard about a resume or how things will look to a future boss. Screw 'em, right? You behaved long enough. Now is the time to make your own rules and let somebody else worry about pleasing you.

JOURNAL, WEEK 9-10
Saint Vincent to Jougne, France

Monday, 3/9/15--Saint Vincent to Nus (Aosta)

I've been watching weather forecasts for Aosta Valley and was a little worried about highs in the teens and twenties Fahrenheit. It's turning into a beautiful week, though. Those 15-17F mornings have grown into 30F afternoons that feel like 40. With the sun shining on the valley, I'm not complaining.

The valley is also filled with smokey haze from noon onward. They burn lots of firewood here even on mild days, and lots of farmers are cleaning brush out of vineyards now as well. Add that to the industrial smoke and the high pressure system sitting on us, and it makes for a hazy place.

I stopped at Nus today, 12k shy of Aosta. A stazione was handy, so I took the train on into the city so that I could have the same hotel for an extra night.

Tuesday, 3/10/15--Nus to Aosta

Got up early for the train back to Nus to finish the walk to Aosta. Found a beautiful nature trail beside the river, squeezed in between highways and business strips. It made for a sweet, quiet walk. Arrived by noon, but I'm still taking an extra rest day tomorrow to take care of business online and do some other errands. My pack has gotten heavier bit by bit, and I have a few things I pack in expectation of having to stay in lots of hostels. That's not proving to be the case, so it's time to purge some weight and bulk.

Wednesday, 3/11/15--rest day in Aosta

After walking every day for 10 straight (even though some were fairly short routes), it feels nice to sleep in an extra half hour and to be able to walk for breakfast without dragging the big bag along.

I tracked down info today on where exactly the road is closed up the mountain and how to get through to Switzerland. Got a bus ticket for day after tomorrow. If all goes as planned, I'll walk up to Bosses tomorrow, then back down a k or two to Ertroubles. I'll take the bus Friday morning from there to Orsieres and hope I'll find a safe way to walk on to Martigny from there.

Thursday, 3/12/15--Aosta to Etroubles

It was a hazy day walking north out of Aosta, and I seemed to climb into the haze the farther I walked. The white peaks of the mountains were just suggestions behind the church steeples in every village along the SS 27. It was all up today--no flats or downs. I stayed on the road for most of the way up to Etroubles. The one time I ventured into the woods following Francigena signs, I was quickly up to my knees in "old snow", crusty enough to walk through but tiring. That trail led me into the town just beside the cemetery...just in case, I guess.

Etroubles is the last town of size before the road over the pass is closed. The Napoleon legend continues here...in the centro vecchio, the cluster of stone homes in the middle of town, a plaque on one wall claims the general as an overnight guest when he led his 40,000 troops down the valley in 1800.

My marching has stopped for a day. Since the pass is closed, I'm taking a bus from here through the tunnel to Orsieres on the Swiss side. I'll continue from there to Martigny tomorrow.

Friday--bus from Etroubles to Orsieres

It feels a little like cheating even though my mind tells me it's not. I had a luxurious morning at the hotel, loitering (even slower than lingering) over a big breakfast at the hotel, then shifting to another hotel, The Col Serena) that's next to the bus stop. The Gran San Bernard Express runs twice each day from Aosta to Martigny. Sitting in a warm bus and watching the scenery fly by is so relaxing but also a bit disturbing to know that I'm not getting to see every step of the way "up close and personal" at a walking pace. On the other hand...man, this feels nice to be sitting instead of walking.

The road down from the tunnel to Orsieres is a ribbon of switchbacks, several tight enough that the bus straddles both lanes to make the turns. Our bus is 10 minutes behind schedule, but I'm happy that our driver isn't working to make up the time on the downhill. Several of those turns look out over a long, straight drop down to rocks below.

I sat down to lunch as soon as I hit town. I'd planned to

stay the night, but the weather was so nice that I decided to walk an hour to Sembrancher. To fuel up I ordered the prix fixe menu at a cafe. Sticker shock set in as it was a third again as expensive as the lunch menus in Italy. In Italy that was 3 courses plus a little "coffeecito" for $12 or so. Here it's 3 big courses of heavy Germanic food (salad, sausages, potatoes with cream sauce, great bread, cake with raspberry sauce) for $22. More sticker shock. And waistline shock. (I had a handful of cashews and a glass of wine for dinner.)

I realized I had no trail map for this country, so I stopped to ask for help at the local tourism office. The women there were very helpful and dug out a trail plan for me. MShe said the Francigena route through the woods was pretty and "easy to follow".

I should have known, right? 90 minutes later I stumbled down off the mountain, exhausted from climbing and slogging through snow, only 3k down the road to La Douay. I was feeling like a proper ijit for losing the markers and climbing too high. To add to the insult, as I'm huffing and struggling WAY up too high, I turn a corner and meet a guy, older than me, pushing his Mom UP the mountain in a wheelchair...out for their afternoon stroll, smiling like it was the easiest thing in the world. Pissed me off actually. Not good for tourist relations in my opinion. I would have complained to the tourist lady except that the guy gave me directions to get my butt down out of the woods. Then smiled and waved and strolled on UP the mountain. Smartass.

The good news is that I did find a gîte...a kind of French B&B that had a sweet warm bar/restaurant attached (Alpine flavor) where I could spend the night. It also featured a rushing stream outside my window...made me want to get up and pee all night.

Saturday--3/14/15
(Pi Day of the Century)

La Douay to Martigny

Easy Start, hard finish. There's a small paved road that winds along in the shadow of the elevated highway from La Douay to Sembrancher, and it was nice wandering through the trees, hearing the river, not watching traffic. Sembrancher sits on a 90-degree bend in the river valley and is built on an old farming and trading post. Ancient timbered barns, many converted to homes, lined my way into the town center.

The colorful green and blue trail signs for La Vie Francigene, the French version of the name, are labeled as trail 70 here. Those signs lead me across the train tracks to the uphill side of the rails, but the map I have showed the trail as staying low, down near those tracks. It's a liar. The map is a damned liar. What started as a flat road across gentle green meadows, sprinkled here and there with picturesque bits of pristine white snow, soon lead me up to mountain-goat heaven, high enough and with sharp enough drops to make me have to concentrate pretty hard on walking. Then, to make things interesting, a bit of ice and slick snow start showing up on that high route. Step wrong on a slick spot, and you're in for a quick ride to the bottom.

That's how they suck you in on this Francigene trail...lead you just a little ways up the hill until you're too far along to go back, then drag you up so high you could look down on your cholesterol levels. Kind of like heroin dealers, I guess...give you a taste to get you started, and then you're stuck.

What came next almost did me in. Just before I was due to hit a town for a break, I came to a big snow avalanche that completely blocked me. Going back would take me back over the high icy parts, so I had to bushwhack down through the worst briars and thorns of the trip to get down to where I could ford another cold river. By the time I reached the other side, I felt like I'd been mugged. I'd had thoughts of getting so hung up in Bre'r Rabbit's briar patch that I'd just get stuck there...would be a skeleton someone would find years later and think, "Hmmm...I wonder what this old fart was doing trying to walk through briars like this?!" I washed the mud and blood off and stopped soon after for a coffee, but I must have still looked bad. The bar owner gave me my cafe au lait for free. Now, she may have been flirting with me, but...nahhh...I just looked that bad. She wished me "Bon chance" as I left, so I must have looked like I was going to need some luck.

Sunday, 3/15/17. Ides of March

Martigny to Saint-Maurice

What a change from yesterday! A welcome change. My trail on the map ran off the page at the edge of Martigny, and I didn't even look for a new map. I found some flat paved roads than run through the valley and am really enjoying a calm, quiet walk. No rockslides, no avalanches, no briars. So far.

This valley features some fairly large farms, but the space between those is is chopped into tiny little parcels of roughly a quarter-acre, each with its own little "garden house". Some of these are rough sheds, but many are carefully and artistically designed as weekend cabins. Today many were being tended busily by owners.

Arrived in Saint-Maurice mid-afternoon and found a room in a hotel run by the Franciscans. A choir from Kings College Cambridge was also here, warming up for an afternoon performance at the local abbey. I'd hoped to hear a bit of that concert as well as a tango concert later in the evening. I was moving too slowly to catch the choir, and when I found out that tango tickets were $70, I realized I was more of a $14.75 fan than a $70 one.

Tomorrow-- down the valley toward Aigle and Lac Leman!

Monday, 3/16/15--Saint-Maurice to Aigle

Another day of easy, safe, flat walking through the valley. There is more industry and industrial farms here than the small-holdings I saw yesterday. There is also enough wind blowing up the valley from the lake to warrant an occasional windmill/generator.

Was moving slowly (contentedly) and so arrived late at Villeneuve, a pretty lake town on the east tip of Lac Leman. All three hotels were priced toward business expense-account travelers, so I backtracked a k or two to take advantage of a motel I'd passed coming into town. I could have pushed on another 5k into Montreux, but I'll save that last happy bit for tomorrow morning when I can really enjoy it.

Tuesday, Wednesday, 3/17&18/15--Villeneuve to Montreux

The day is just as nice as I'd hoped--sunny, still, cool--a perfect day to stroll the lakefront into town. Montreux and the communities around it have all invested in manicuring the waterfront into one long (more than 20k), rambling, tree-lined garden. Even now, early in the spring, the walks are filled with blooms and color. They're also filled with people--walkers, joggers, sitters, even a unicycle or two. The floral plan worked...people appreciate this space and use it.

Early on my rest day, I took the cable-train up a steep 1/5k track up to Glion. The two cars help counter-weight each other with one coming down while the other goes up. They pass in the middle of the route at the only "bump" in the track that's widened for two. Glion is directly up the mountain above Montreux and Territet. There are steps up in case you'd like to walk it. Do that every day and you could let go of that gym membership.

There is a Cafe de la Gare at the top of the rail as there is at almost every station in Switzerland. These range from bare-bones waiting rooms for trains to fantastic terrasse cafes with a panoramic view like this one. I sat out with my chocolat chaud and soaked up the sun like an old tomcat. I hadn't been drifting there for long when a family from Galway settled in and caught the same inertia virus I had. After I offered to play photographer for the balcony shot, Mickey and Mary and daughter, Claire and I became fast friends. Claire teaches in one of the many private schools that fill the Swiss towns on the north shore of the lake. She was on a month holiday, so Mickey and Mary had come to spend a week checking out the place. We wished each other a Happy St. Paddy's Week, and I left them in charge of the terrace.

Thursday, 3/19/15. Montreux to Vevey

Well, it was supposed to be Montreux to Lausanne, 28k, but I only made it a lazy 10. The day was too perfect, the walk too beautiful to hurry through. When I happened on a cheap (relatively so) hostel/hotel on the lake in Vevey, I took it as a sign that I should stop and absorb more of the lake. Tomorrow is time enough reach Lausanne and turn inland again.

Besides, I kept bumping into more and more notes, sculptures, paintings about composers who thrived in this area. I mentioned The Shelleys and Lord Byron before. (Frankenstein)

Igor Stravinsky wrote part of the Rite of Spring at Clarens (according to locals, at least). Richard Strauss wrote Metamorphosis here. Hindemith worked here beside the lake. Freddie Mercury made Montreux his studio-home for part of the year.

Nina Simone, an American pianist-turned-singer, was an activist in the civil rights movement in the 1960's. She'd been a student at Julliard in New York but had to leave for financial reasons. In the late 60's she grew tired of the racial situation in the US and left to live abroad. By the time she died in 2003, she had become known throughout the Western world. The spread through the Internet of the live recording of her performance at the 1976 Montreux Jazz Festival has won her many younger fans.

Igor Stravinsky, as I mentioned, is also remembered for the time he spent near Lac Leman. While passing through Montreux this time, I stayed in a youth hostel. (Yes, they let old dudes stay there, too.) I barely noticed the musical notation-decorations that covered one wall of a break room at the hostel. On the last morning I was there for breakfast, I stopped to have a closer look. I realized it was a real tune and not just the use of some cute little eighth notes. The theme was part of the Rite of Spring that locals claim he composed while living at Clarens, next door to Montreux. (The Stravinsky Foundation states that he finished the piece while still in Russia, before leaving in 1914 to avoid the coming war.) The piece is a ballet and was choreographed by Nijinsky. The tale depicts a pagan ritual, and the musical style was such that it caused fights among the audience at its premiere in Paris in 1913.

Musicians have long been used to hearing that story, but try to imagine today your own local concert hall. What would it take, what sounds would have to occur onstage to cause you and your peers to be outraged enough to fight over a performance?

One more musician inspired by this lake area—Freddie Mercury of Queen. Though he worked most of his life in the UK, he also kept a studio here at Montreux for part of his life. A statue by Czech sculptress Irena Sedlecka is a focal point of the Place du Marche' on the waterfront in the city.

The Vevey Hotel &Guesthouse turned out to be a nice combination hostel/hotel, and I had a bright, sunny corner room. Was able to sit on their 4th floor terrasse and work the afternoon. Went to see Insurgent at the cinema around the corner. Ehhh...

Friday, 3/20/15--Vevey to Lausanne

In walking mode today, and it was a day to make anyone want to walk. Once again I didn't bother to look for any official trail and instead just walked the lakefront. Here is a sidewalk beside Rt. 9 that follows the shore all the way to Lausanne. The lake was still and hazy, a silver-gray that completely erased the mountains on the south shore of the lake. Evian was hidden behind the mirror of the lake.

On the other side of the highway, stacked to the north are the grapevine terraces of the Lavaux region. The dull brown stone walls march up the hillside, and many were being worked today. Vines were being trimmed and strung to the wires that lace the fields. Piles of brush and weeds were stacked and smoldering in the cool morning air. The taste of woodsmoke followed me to a cafe in a green park by the lake at Rivaz. Cully and Pully were spaced along the road like steps into Lausanne, where I'd not found a hotel. I thought I'd find cheap options, but I'd forgotten how upscale the city is. I sat to sulk over lunch at 3pm, and then started walking again.

It's easy to get lost in the architecture of the city. Lausanne is built like the rows of terraces that flank it on either side by the lake. Almost every street of the city from the lake toward the north is a bit higher than the one before. Some are as high as the roofs of the lower homes.

Late afternoon I happened on a sign for a guesthouse similar to the one in Vevey. The counter staff were seriously happy people, and it lifted my mood to meet them. Most of the customers in these hostels are backpacking 20-somethings, but there were half a dozen guys there that were as "mature" as I am. I stayed in a 4-bed dorm but only had one roomie, a German-born English teacher from Basel. Jan was in town for a single-day workshop and preferred the hostel at $40 for a bed instead of the hotel prices that started at $100. The other older guests were all working stiffs, too, who didn't mind the closer quarters of the dorms in order to save some money.

A decent panang curry rounded out the day.

Saturday, 3/21/15--Lausanne to La Sarraz

Rain today...the first time in three weeks. I'd planned to avoid walking in the rain, but I'd had such a lucky long stretch of sunshine that I felt ready again for a moist walk. Besides which, this "rain" was more a suggestion of moisture rather than a hard, soaking downpour that's more frequent at home. I'd pre-booked a pizzeria/hotel in La Sarraz and made it in time to sample the house specialty for lunch--ham, onion, mushrooms, Gruyere cheese, olives, tomatoes, heavily dosed with cracked black pepper. Worth the walk.

Now to decide the next stop. One listing of suggested routes turns toward Lake Neuchatel and Yverdons-les-

Bains, but that road will keep me in country another couple of nights. I think I'm ready to move on to France and the kinder, gentler Euro. There's another road that will put me across the border tomorrow night, and I can rejoin the "real" Francigena the next day at Pontarlier, France. Will be studying maps tonight.

The rain is ending, and there's sun on the prediction for tomorrow. I may get lucky again.

Sunday, 3/22/15--La Sarraz to Jounge, France

What a difficult, interesting, beautiful, hard day of walking. I left town this morning wanting to make it to France, feeling a bit beat up financially by the Swiss franc. Didn't know if I could make it the 27k up into the mountains to Jougne, and didn't know if I could find a place to stay if I did make it. (Some of the smaller hotels like I search for have great websites, some have defective ones, and many don't bother.) Also didn't know what kind of walking path I'd find since I was leaving behind the marked trails.

As soon as I left the hotel, I knew I'd miscalculated. I left in two layers of shirts and a cap. Hadn't made it out of town before I had to stop and dress for winter. It was 35F with a hard north wind in my face. Sunday morning, so not any real traffic to worry about, and that was good. When the wind is strong, it grabs my backpack and wants to throw me in the ditch. I start to lean into it, but then when it suddenly stops, I lurch...right into a traffic lane.

I was cussin' and spittin' at it this morning, but the way itself was a pretty one. I'm climbing up into the Juras, but the climb is about taking one rolling hill after another. There were no windbreaks for the first 7k, so when I walked into the village of Croy, I was ready to thaw out.

I did find a great cafe open in Croy, and they were happy to sell me a cafe au lait and let me warm up. The family that ran the place had just sat down to eat an early lunch before their Sunday mid-day rush. Papa was working a crossword puzzle, older brother was focused on his food, and younger brother had his eyes down on his food. I was the only customer in the place, and they left me to my reading and writing and my grand creme, a large hot coffee.

I sat for awhile and pondered how lucky I am to be able to wander in and out of the weather on an early spring Sunday morning in the Swiss Jura Mountains. Lucky to have the coin to be able to see these quaint old off-the-road villages and to stop wherever I want to drink a coffee by a warm stove and listen to the French chatter around me, to have to lift my feet when the Madam comes by with her mop and tells me that now I'll have to sit till the floor dries. (Oh, darn.) it's one of those luckiest-guy-in-the-world kind of days...until I get back up and face the road and wind again. Then I'll go right back to cussin' and spittin'.

I did make it to Vallorbe, the last town of size on the Swiss highway 9. Was able to warm up again over lunch and decided I could do another 7k to Jougne. It was a steady uphill grind from lunch, but the wind abated and the temp rose 5 or 6 degrees. That plus the heat of climbing made the walk easier. I crossed the border, watching the Swiss border guards checking everyone coming in but ignoring those of us heading to France. At the French post 100 yards farther along...nothing. No one was home. I walked on past the first cafe and immediately felt better. Their prices were posted in the window and were a third cheaper than in Switzerland. It's not that I'm cheap, but...well, yes, maybe I am a cheap bastard.

The road continued up the mountain, and up...and up. I passed the base of a ski lift and began to find more and more patchy snow. My luck was good again this afternoon when I hit Jougne (finally) at 5pm. One of the first buildings I saw was an inviting 2-star Hotel de la Poste with a neon blue "Ouverte" sign. I felt like I'd earned my hot shower and a meal, and the bar is calling to me to find some antifreeze.

It's good to make it to a third country. Vive la France!

JOURNAL, WEEK 11-12
FRANCE

I missed on judging the weather again this morning. Left the room all bundled up again and immediately had to stop and lose the warm hat and windbreaker, pulling out the cap and shoes. Another bright, bright blue sky, and the 34 degrees felt like 44. A really nice day to walk down the mountain. Of course, almost any day is a good one for heading downhill.

The road--mostly France's highway N57--heads north through a thick evergreen forest. I left the ski slopes behind, but not the snow. Both sides of the road were packed with white on green, and a snowmelt creek followed me down the hill, chattering the whole way.

Tuesday, 3/24/15--Pontarlier to Lods

I'm not a Courbet aficionado, but yesterday I walked from Pontarlier to Lods, near the source of the Loue River, and found another connection to Montreux and Lac Leman. Around midday I found signs telling me I was in the Pays de Courbet, the region that was home to the 19th Century realist painter Gustave Courbet.

I left Pontarlier across fields ready for planting, got to spend an hour or two climbing through an evergreen forest still packed with patches of late snow, and exited those woods onto more fields. The men driving tractors that were spreading composted manure--smelling disturbingly similar to Eau de Pilgrim--all waved as they passed. I think they kind of enjoy slinging the stuff all around the lone hiker walking their roads.

I'd started enjoying walking these relatively flat fields, thinking that I've probably left most of the dramatic Alpine-type scenery behind me. I was OK with that as these fields and farms have their own appeal. About that time, though, the road suddenly descended into another dark wood. I turned a corner and there just ahead of me was a stunning valley, the "Source of the Loue"...the birth of the river that cuts its way to Besancon.

It felt like I'd stumbled into Jurassic Park, or maybe Shangri-La. For my Arkansas friends, think of the sight you have driving down into Steel Creek, but twice as deep. It's a breath-taking feeling to pass that dark rock wall (decorated with an urn of flowers memorializing someone who died there) and emerge onto the brink of that immense canyon. Another turn half a kilometer down the road squeezes through a shaft cut between stone pillars and leads to the valley that's home to Mouthier-Haute-Pierre.

The village is itself stuck to a rock halfway down from the top of the gorge. The river is bright green as it shoots through the hydroelectric facilities below the town. The place was quiet as I walked through, with not even a little bar open to offer me a coffee. I slumped on down the road toward Lods, the next village in line. It's too early for river fun yet, but the signs for canoe rentals, swimming areas, and trout fishing hide in the trees beside my road.

Found a place to sleep 2k down the hill at Lods, another "Petite Cite' Comtoise de Caractere", a designation that the town is one of the region's places of special character. The Hotel de France is an old one, and I'm (once again) the only guest. In the dining room tonight it was just me and the family...mom and pop with the two 30-something married kids and their cute toddler daughter. I missed lunch (remember the dates and cashews...). Never even had a chance for a coffee all day, so I made up for it tonight. Entree was a sweet coleslaw with slices of local saucissons (a kind of salami) and great country bread, main plate was a thick chunk of ham, a big piece of local sausage, fresh green beans, and new potatoes. (Did I mention the fresh bread?)

Had a nice light banana/yogurt "Berliner" (yogurt banana pudding?) for dessert...not my favorite, but not bad. No cognac tonight, but a drop of local kirsch. I'm heading to bed happy...if I can sit up awhile longer to digest.

Wednesday, 3/25/15--Lods to past Ornans (the"Marsieres Bifurcation")

A bit of rain, mostly "heavy cloud", but this is a beautiful walk through the valley next to the Loue River. Had a big lunch (Lapin au sauce de moutarde ancienne), then caught the bus on into Besancon for a few nights at the youth hostel Les Oiseaux.

Thursday, 3/26/15

Couldn't get an early bus back out to my continuation point to finish the walk into town, so I covered the distance in the opposite direction, walking out of Besancon down through the Foret Communale de Besancon to Tarcenay. Beautiful, gray day...cool. Stopped to warm my hands by a the lunchtime fire of a wood-cutting crew in the woods. Two groups of men were sitting together having lunch, and the only woman on the crew sat by herself at the fire.

Friday, 3/27/15

A day off in Besancon. Nice! I bought a day pass on the bus/metro for €4.20 and made a tour of the city. At dinner I met Ansel and Ginny Ogle, friends from Arkansas who are living in nearby Belfort for a year of teaching. We went for drinks, and they took me to their friends' house for dinner. Catherine and Serge (teaching supervisor and architect) served a "winter meal" of four cold sliced meats, boiled potatoes, green salad, and Mont D'Or cheese. Catherine cut a plug from the center of the round of cheese, filled it with local white wine, then heated the cheese in the oven until the top was browned and crisped. They finished with beignets topped with a compote of mixed fresh fruits and a shot of kirsch from Mouthier-Haute Pierre. Nice people, and a great meal.

Saturday, 3/28/15. Besancon to Cussey-sur-L'Ognon

Rain was forecast for the afternoon and the coming week. Not a fun prospect, but so be it. I couldn't find a likely spot for a stop at 20k, so I stopped at Cussey. Felt like going on, but the rain was starting, no bus lines were around, and the next hotel was 20k out. Tiny little place, but there was an artisanal boulangerie next door and a pizza joint up the street.

When I walked up to the pizza joint a block away, I stopped for a second to look at a map on my phone just as an older woman (even older than the guy pushing Ma up the mountain in the chair), chatting to herself, obviously on the way somewhere. She saw me, asked "Ca va bien?", and leaned in for a neighbor's cheek-kisses like we were old buddies. I assured her I was OK, asked after her, and she just laughed and answered ...something...as she walked on by. Made me laugh. Then, the three 30-something guys running the pizza joint were laughing and cutting up with everyone who came through. Steady stream of takeout customers, and all of them knew the guys. They're the only game in town on a rainy Saturday night except for the upscale restaurant at my auberge. I was the only sit-down customer and got a great Franche-Comptoir salad...almost like my meal last night...big bed of lettuce and tomatoes, topped with hot sliced new potatoes and sliced local sausage, served with a melted white cheese as a topping. Good eats!

Sunday, 3/29/15--Cussey to Gy

As forecast, rain. Blowing, drippy rain for the 20k to Gy. Fortunately, my route was on a tiny unused road through the Monts de Gy, another forest. Beautiful way, but not a dry place to sit and rest all day. I was knackered by the time I reached Gy, and the one hotel was quiet. Seemed open, but no one answered. I finally had a sit-down at the one bar in town and sucked on a coffee. Tasted great, as only a hot coffee after a wet 20k walk can. She threw me out at closing time--1:30--and I lucked into finding the hotel open.

It was the only thing in town that was, other than the marie, the town hall. Today was the local departmental elections, so a trickle of folks found their way in to vote. I was hoping to find the pizzeria down the block open for Sunday supper, but no such luck. I had to settle for a tiny tin of bad tuna (ugly sauce, anyway), an apple, and some chocolate for dinner in my room. I guess I could have dined downstairs in the hotel's breakfast room or living room as apparently I was the only living person in the place...no other guests or staff around that night. After a day in the wind and rain, though, I felt lucky to have a warm, dry room, dry clothes, and a soft bed. We've all had tougher nights than that one.

I lost an hour today, by the way to the French version of "spring forward, fall back". I thought my watch was on the fritz until I checked online. Their change happens on the last Sunday in March, and the locals don't appear to like it any more than we do.

Monday, 3/30/15--Gy to Gray

Forecasters got it right again, but I did have a lucky dry first hour. Stopped to rest in a covered bus stop and got lucky again--I was sitting and sheltered while the first hard rain of the day blew through. I caught a few later ones (or rather they caught me), but it was nice to miss one. Also felt luckier than the previous day to find another covered shelter in an old wash house down the road for a later rest. Some of the village wash shelters are elaborate stone and timber structures that have survived for hundreds of years. They're not used for washing now, but they're maintained as local monuments. And, they make a nice covered place to kick off your boots and get out of the weather for a break.

Gray is a larger town that's known for it's location on the Saone River and for its proliferation of schools and colleges. I was just happy they had cafes that served more than tuna and apples.

Tuesday, 3/31/15--Gray to Champlitte

The weather called for 20mph wind and rain today, and I did not want to walk another 20k in it. Losing my spizz for that kind of walk. When I finished breakfast, though, it was momentarily dry. Windy, but dry. I figured I better make the most of the dry. It didn't last long, but the wind did. Half the day was windy, the other half was windy and wet--hard blowing rain on the left side of my head all day.

I made it to Champlitte, though, and lucked into another inexpensive 2-star hotel. Another hot shower, a nap, and hot coffee, and all is right again.

Wednesday, 4/1/15.
(Will they celebrate April Fool's here?)
Champlitte to Longeau-Percey

Ah...Wednesday was supposed to be my mid-week break in the weather...cloudy and windy, instead of rainy and windy. My first step out the door--the very first step, actually--the rain started. The wind never stopped--dead in my face all day. The rain varied from drizzle to mist to real rain...then to sleet mixed with snow, a bit of hail, and a few times some bursts of ice pellets. Just when I was thinking it was time for spring temps, I froze most of the day.

Found a great warm cafe and overate for lunch. It was nice to warm up.. Made the last 10k of my 25k to Longeau-Percey on a full belly, anyway.

The little hotel I found--L'Espace--was run by an Asian lady and her 20-something daughter. I was the only overnight guest (again), which probably explains why the other two hotels in this little town were both closed. They were both solicitous and wanted me to be happy, so what the place lacked in amenities--which was a lot-- they made up for in attention. For breakfast Thursday morning I even had an omelette made to order. This was a real treat after many breakfasts of just bread and coffee. Bread and butter and jam. And bread. More bread.

Thursday, 4/2/15--Longeau to Langres

I stumbled in a daze a short day up to the edge of Langres. Didn't have much in me today and need a day completely off. May try to take one when I get to Chaumont. For now this was an easy 12k up the road, hardly enough to break a sweat. Helping in that cause was once again a hard, steady, 12mph wind. The temp is 39F, which makes it feel...well, brisk. Just as I arrived, the misty fog changed to blowing, drizzling, cold rain. I had planned to wander Langres a bit as it is one of the towns on Sigeric's list of stops from a thousand years ago. So far, though, nothing about this weather day makes me inclined to step outside again. Two more days of this predicted, and then I'm supposed to see the sun again.

A side note--today I walked near Bourg, France, a village I'd not heard of before today. Out on the D974 highway, a country road, stands a monument to General George S. Patton, the famous US military leader. The monument also claims that Bourg is the birthplace of the U.S. Army's Tank Corps. Several sources I checked confirm that this was indeed the place where in 1918 General Patton set about training the first large-scale armored division in the Army.

The story is also told of Patton returning to the area in later years and finding that the town had maintained since 1918 the grave of an unknown soldier. Patton, not remembering that any of his men were buried there, checked the "grave" only to find that it was an old military latrine that US soldiers had jokingly marked with a cross and the legend "Abandoned Rear". Local citizens had mistaken the mound for a fresh grave and maintained it to honor the soldiers who had been stationed there. Patton confirms the story in his memoirs.

Friday, 4/3/15--Langres to Vesaignnes-sur-Marne (Chaumont)

Finally, a calm, relatively dry day. I had a feeling Langres was going to be an interesting town and wish I'd had weather for walking it yesterday. It took almost two hours starting out today to wander the 2k through Langres. It's one of the towns on Sigeric's list, which makes it at least a thousand years old. Some of the city ramparts remain, several interesting churches, parks...I would enjoy spending more time there.

As I was leaving town a couple stopped me to chat. They weren't carrying packs, but it was apparent they were pilgrims. They had that tired, weathered, happy look to them. It turns out Dominique and Jean-Luc are not on he Via Francigena but are on their way to Spain and then Portugal. This town is a crossroads where these two major pilgrimages meet.

They'd left home in Nancy 10 days ago and had arrived yesterday in Langres. We had a chat on the road, swapped photos, and moved on. It made me happy to see another couple of walkers even if they are on a different route.

My day was an easy one until I took a left through the village of Chanoy. My map showed an easy return to the road after the village, but as often happens, the map was wrong. It dumped me onto a dead-end dirt road on the wrong side of a fenced toll road. I had to climb a barbed wire fence, slog through a small swamp, then cut across somebody's boggy pasture looking for a way back onto a road. After that, it was a cinch to reach Vesaignes-sur-Marne in time to catch a bus to Chaumont for a hotel. Will return tomorrow to continue walking.

SINGING THE MORNING

I heard it again this morning from a dozen or more strangers, and I admit, I've grown to like it.

The French don't say [use italics] their "Good morning" so much as sing it. "Bonjour Monsieur". It's delivered with a lilt and changing pitch that really is musical.

Today I was having a morning coffee in the old center of Chaumont, the eastern French city that sits in a bend of the Marne River. I happened to be at a table near the door, but it wouldn't have mattered. Everyone who walked through the door greeted everyone in the bar with that song,"Bonjour, Monsieur. Bonjour, Madame." And everyone in the cafe mumbles or or at least nods a return to the greeting. Local or stranger, it doesn't matter--everyone greets, and everyone is greeted. The bartender is the choirmaster and leads the response. Her response is clear and strong enough that it feels like an admission ticket, a French "Welcome to the club!"

It's as if we're all in Cheers, and every single person through the door is Norm.

The failure to recognize this simple practice of "greeting the room" in European bars, stores, restaurants, is one of the things that marks Americans as foreigners and might invite locals to be a slight bit less friendly to us. After all, from their point of view, how hard could it be to say "Good morning" when you walk in a room? But because Americans don't know to do this or are too embarrassed/shy/whatever to try the unfamiliar words, they may come across as less friendly with the first step in the door.

Chaumont isn't a big city, and this particular bar I was in today was a local hangout. Bar/cafes here are that above all else--a place to see your neighbors, to be seen, to collect the news, to make sure the world is still spinning as it was yesterday. It was obvious here that the couple behind the bar really did know almost everyone through the door. I was an exception, but because I knew the password, I was given the congregation's blessing and smiles.

To open the door when leaving, the magic words aren't "Open sesame", but "Merci, Madame, au revoir!", at which point the door practically opens itself and the room calls a general chorus of "Au revoir, merci Monsieur, bonne journee", etc. There's no sermon or special music, but the more I hear this the more it rises closer to the level of a religious ritual.

At my second bar of the morning...(It was a tough day!)...I was at the bar on the bottom floor of my hotel, the quaint little Hotel Le Royal just a few blocks south of the gare. The couple that run the hotel also man the bar. Again, it's a local crowd. The jokes and personal comments were added to the "Bonjour" before some men (an all-male crowd today) were through the door. In this bar, though, as in others, everyone who knows the password gets a handshake as well. Everyone who came in made the rounds to the half-dozen patrons and shook our hands. I got the formal polite word, but others got growled or grunted comments and jokes that made it feel like a relaxed small-town Saturday morning would feel in most parts of the world.

The sweetest part of the song this morning, though, was the grandfather who came in with a young boy, maybe ten years old. The man was first in the door, greeting us all, then started the round of handshakes. The grandson had clearly been initiated, following his grandfather to every table, looking everyone in the eye, shaking every hand. They moved to the bar and repeated the steps with everyone standing there, the boy standing on tiptoes to reach across and shake hands with the owner. The man got his coffee, the boy got his chocolat chaud, and they stood at the bar catching up on the neighborhood news.

No one made a big deal out this...which made it more touching to me. The room accepted the boy as one of the gang, including him in some conversations and ignoring him at times. I felt like I was in a secret club meeting and had gotten a chance to see the next generation being handed the keys to the strongbox.

The singing doesn't stop with "Good morning", either. French is a musical language, and it is sung throughout the day. When a server delivers a coffee, it's arranged just so on the table, with the handle of the cup turned to the right, the spoon placed carefully, and then pronounced as perfect with "E voila, Monsieur!"

When food is brought to the table for lunch or dinner, it's always served with a side order of "Bon appetit!" Sung, you understand, not spoken. The food isn't finally flavored until every one of the staff who passes the table--and often other cafe patrons as well-- offer the blessing, "Bon appetit". It may be as reflexive as an American's "bless you!" response to a sneeze, but I don't think so. I like to believe the words are born from the country's love of food and their respect for cooking as an art form.

Maybe that's just a happy traveler's romanticizing of a country's habit, but I invite you to listen closer to the songs the next time you're serenaded. Be bold and join the chorus when you walk into the cafe. Give them your own "Bonjour" and see who sings along. You don't have to actually genuflect, but the words alone have power that say "I see you, I respect this place, and I respect you."

[A postscript on singing: As I passed through Besancon, I took a day to rest and rode trams through the city. The new tram system there features recorded voices announcing stops. These voices, though, aren't the standard, generic telephone-operator's voice. The system opted to have a variety of men, women, and children's voices programmed to "sing the stations" to us. It's a sweet surprise to tram travelers.]

Saturday, 4/4/15 Chaumont

Rain, wind, cold for the day into Chaumont

Easter Sunday, 4/5/15. Chaumont to Colombey les Deux Eglises

Was startled by the weather today. Walked out the door of my Hotel Le Royal in Chaumont and saw an odd color up above. Looked it up in a dictionary and found out it's called "blue". Sometimes the sky in parts of the world is this color, but I haven't seen it in awhile.

I walked through the closed, quiet carnival rides ('cause nothing says "Easter" like shooting galleries and fried carny food) and down beneath the XIIth Century fortress and started climbing again immediately up into a strong northeast wind. The sky may be blue, but the other side of my face was going to be frozen today. Somehow it doesn't bother as much when there's no rain or ice pellets blowing up your snout.

I passed three little towns on the 26k road to Colombey, hoping for a hot coffee in each. No such luck. Unlike in Italy, where there seems to be a bar/cafe in every burg, the folks in these places made their own coffee at home. I settled for rest breaks wherever I could find a dry, sunny spot out of the wind...against someone's front wall, leaning on an old church in a cemetery in one village, and huddled against the back wall of a little stone bus stop an hour before my target. Once out of the wind,I had a great day of walking through rolling hills of new green hay and soybeans.

Colombey les Deux Eglises does indeed have two churches, an ancient one and a new one only three hundred years old. It's behind the "new" church, I learned as I entered town, that Charles DeGaulle is buried. Most of the history I'm finding along the way is "accidental education" for me as I'm picking roads based on distance and direction rather than the treasures they link.

The signs here inform that this was DeGaulle's last home. He was here when he died in 1970, and the town has memorialized him with a hilltop memorial, preserving his gravesite behind the tiny church, and by opening his home, Le Boisserie, as a museum. Small gift shops, cafes, hotels, and champagne cellars mark the town as a tourist destination French citizens visit in tribute to the general who led the Free French forces as the Allies reclaimed the country after the Normandy invasion. An imposing 100-foot "Croix Lorainne", the symbol of the French Resistance, stands out above the trees on the highest point of the village, next to the DeGaulle Memorial.

DEATH ON THE TRAIL

Headline announcing the death of a Spanish pilgrim in the spring of 2015:

'No quería matarla, pero la golpeé'
("I didn't want to kill her, but I hit her.")

Death is a function of history, and it surrounds us on the trail. The very fact of the age of the pilgrimage means that succeeding generations have had centuries to erect monuments and memorials to those who have come before.

Many of these remembrances are tributes, heralding the courage or historical importance of a hero. Others are vast holding pens for the remains of the fallen in the world's wars. The Francigena in France wanders through the Somme and Marne valleys, and the incredible numbers of victims of World War I and II meant that they had to be left behind, their graves marked with countless rows of white crosses in military cemeteries.

The immediacy of death is also our companion as we walk the pilgrimage routes, whether they lead to Santiago or Rome or some other distant target. While many of the trails are safe ways through wilderness and civilization, some are more hazardous mountain routes, particularly in extreme weather.

Even though most days en route are filled with the the lightness of spirit common to hikers anywhere, we're reminded of our mortality--sometimes even in our moments of greatest joy-- by the presence of tiny memorials erected beside the trail remembrances of pilgrims who died in isolated places.

The message at the head of this chapter was the end of a sad story of the murder of a pilgrim on the Spanish trail, El Camino de Santiago. The connections of that trail with the Francigena are numerous, and most of the hikers of the French Route have also walked to Santiago. The community of pilgrims on the European trails is large and growing yearly. In recent years more than 100,000 walk all or part of the Spanish trail. Many are moved to stay connected to other pilgrims through social media.

In April, when I had just crossed over the Juras into the southeast of France, I received an email from Ivar, a hiker who manages one of the many pilgrim websites, this one on Facebook (the Camino de Santiago Forum). He sent out a blanket note to his list of subscribers, asking for help locating a lost pilgrim.

Dear Cooper,

I am writing since there is a pilgrim missing. It has been several weeks since she was last seen.

I realize that most of you are probably at home, but for those of you on the Camino right now, please read this thread with all the details on this pilgrim:

(A linked website held a plea from a worried brother asking for help in locating his sister, who had disappeared on the Spanish trail.)

I am crossing my fingers that this will help in finding her.

Ivar

The brother of Denise Thiem, an American woman walking alone on the Camino, had written to everyone he could think of to warn that his sister had disappeared near Astorga in northwest Spain. It was early in the season, or else there would probably have been other pilgrims near her who could have helped her through whatever trouble she'd encountered. It had been three weeks since her family had heard from her, however, so the pilgrim network vibrated with the news and with the hope that more eyes on the road could lead to resolution.

Occasional updates throughout the summer revealed no progress in the search, and the outlook turned bleak. Finally, mid-September, a Spanish man who lives near the trail confessed and led police to the body.

There is a death or two on that Spanish trail almost every year, but rarely are these the result of violence. Generally a hiking accident is the cause, or a health-related death. The locals near the Camino are generally supportive of the hikers, providing a safety net that also functions like an unofficial crime-watch effort to prevent abuse of pilgrims.

The thought of death is often with us on the trail, but so is the thought of a richer life. History books are filled with anecdotes of those who have had a brush with death learning to relish their lives more fully. Only by confronting the end do we return to a fuller appreciation of life.

This pilgrimage route is no more or less dangerous than other hikes rated for the general public. As stated before, the Francigena is really a network of routes, and the hikers choose the paths between major points on the trail depending on their own tolerances for risk, comfort, traffic, trail construction, and other factors.

At times on this trail, particularly in high country, I've been on icy trails that made me stop and think, "Whoa...this is one of those places where, if I make a mistake, I could die." A few times the way ahead was dangerous enough, or frozen over, or blocked by snowslide, that I thought about backtracking a few miles in the name of caution. Almost every time, though, stubbornness won out over intelligence, and I found some way to plow ahead or bushwhack around a problem.

These were the moments, though, that made me the happiest. That's after they were done, you understand. Not during. I've learned I have a low tolerance for risk. I'm not the one who's going to climb K2 or sail alone around the world. I'll walk a long trail, but I'll look for the safest one.

The day that comes to mind as I write this was a March morning in the south of Switzerland. Easy start, hard finish. There's a small paved road that winds along in the shadow of the elevated highway from La Douay to Sembrancher, and it was nice wandering through the trees, hearing the river, not watching traffic. Sembrancher sits on a 90-degree bend in the river valley and is built on an old farming and trading post. Ancient timbered barns, many converted to homes, lined my way into the town center.

I had planned to get coffee in town as the morning was a cold one. Clear and cold--a beautiful morning to walk. The bars were either closed or off the trail this morning, though, so I pressed on, thinking that it wouldn't be that far to Bovernier, the next village to the west.

The colorful green and blue trail signs for La Vie Francigene, the French version of the name, are labeled as trail 70 here. Those signs lead me across the train tracks to the uphill side of the rails, but the map I have showed the trail as staying low, down near those tracks. It's a liar. The map is a damned liar. What started as a flat road across gentle green meadows, sprinkled here and there with picturesque bits of pristine white snow, soon lead me up to mountain-goat heaven, high and with sharp enough drops to make me have to concentrate pretty hard on walking. Then, to make things interesting, a bit of ice and slick snow start showing up on that high route. Step wrong on a slick spot, and you're in for a quick ride to the bottom.

That's how they suck you in on this Francigene trail...lead you just a little ways up the hill until you're too far along to go back, then drag you up so high you could look down on your cholesterol levels. Kind of like heroin dealers...give you a taste to get you started, and then you're stuck.

I sweated and wiggled my way past the ice and was happy to feel the trail start winding down toward the river. What came next wasn't as dangerous, but it almost did me in. Just before I was due to hit a town for a big break, I came to a big snow avalanche that completely blocked the path forward. Going back would take me back over the high icy parts, so I had to turn toward the wall of thorn bushes between me and the river. I waded in and had to bushwhack down through the worst briars I'd seen to get down to where I could ford another cold river. By the time I reached the other side, I felt like I'd been mugged. I'd had thoughts of getting so hung up in Bre'r Rabbit's briar patch that I'd just get stuck there...would be a skeleton someone would find years later and think, "I wonder what this old fart was doing trying to walk through briars like this?!" I washed the mud and blood off and stopped soon after for a coffee, but I must have still looked bad. The bar owner gave me my cafe au lait for free. Now, she may have been flirting with me, but...nahhh...I just looked that bad. She wished me "Bon chance" as I left, so I must have looked like I was going to need some luck.

Newly fortified but starting to feel the day, I headed back to the trail toward Martigny, staying closer to a paved road...until it disappeared into a narrow, dark tunnel. I backed and scouted until I spotted a trail over the mountain by way of a steep, narrow path back up toward the ice...at which point I bailed. I hated to be stopped only 2k before Martigny, but I knew I didn't have another icy climb in me. I went backwards 4k to a tiny train depot to get me through that tunnel and the light at the other end, a little hotel in Martigny.

A hot shower and a nap later, I was strolling through a Roman amphitheater, having a coffee at a museum of St. Bernards, and looking for food. I sat down to a dinner of savory crepes, all thoughts of death and dying left behind. Such is the human mind, that once we feel we are out of danger, our thoughts can turn immediately to pleasure. Call it optimism, call it blissful ignorance, whatever...the trail leads forward, and we move on.

JOURNAL, WEEK 13-14-15

Monday, 4/20/15--La Fere to Saint Quentin

Saint Quentin was a pleasant surprise. I knew nothing about this city except that it was on Sigeric's list. It's another strategic hilltop city built around another impressive cathedral. An interesting feature of the church is the frescoed Gregorian chant on the walls of the choir.

A canal off of the Somme through the south side of the centre ville offers a wide promenade and park for runners and walkers. When I arrived on a sunny afternoon, the Grand Place at the ornate Mairie was filled with slow-moving locals, tables at the open cafes were packed, and a track for little folks and the tricycles had been set up in the open center. Spring was making itself felt in the heart of the city.

Tuesday, 4/21/15--Rest day in Saint Quentin

Wednesday, 4/22/15--Saint Quentin to Peronne

As hard as I looked, I couldn't find an easy stopping point for this day, so I pushed the 30k to Peronne. Another town that had escaped my notice, Peronne appeared as another strategic point in this region during the last wars. There is a stone fortress in the center of the town that serves as a museum for the First World War.

It's a walk up a rise into the town, and a father-son team painting their front fence flagged me down as I was nearing the business district. The son had walked part of the Spanish Camino, and like most "veterans" was interested in connecting with other passing pilgrims. They confirmed that the season was early still but that a few of us had begun to drift through. They also told me to be sure to notice the memorial to the Australian soldiers on the north side of town.

Thursday, 4/23/15--Peronne to Bapaume

I passed the Australian war memorial on my way north this morning. It's a small park squeezed between homes on the D1017, but an impressive tribute to Australia's Second Division that captured the important position of Mont St. Quentin in 1918. It was the introduction into the war on the western front for 180,000 Australian soldiers, 60,000 of whom would be killed or injured.

A bar owner had told me that it was for this reason that Australian visitors to the area are numerous and are specially welcomed. On this night and several others I heard that distinct accent around me in the cafes.

Friday, 4/24/15--Bapaume to Arras
SACRED SPACES

The land is flatter now, gently rolling. There are fewer vineyards and more fields of mustard. The rain played tag with me part of the day but not enough to be bothersome. I was on the outskirts of Arras for an hour before I finally reached my bed for the night. I hiked another 2k on into the center of town to find dinner and maybe a movie, but I settled for food.

I got delayed around the Place des Heros, the plaza in front of the ornate Hotel de Ville, by an amazing photography display commemorating the beginning of the Grand Guerre, the First World War. One hundred photos from that event have been enlarged and mounted outdoors on the square. They give a glimpse into the lives of some of the men and women involved in the war near Arras. Soldiers from many different countries came to fight, and the exhibit shows a bit of the courage and enthusiasm on their arrival as well as the devastation that resulted from the war.

I'd spent the past weeks walking past military cemeteries, rows of white crosses seeing to grow inside the stone walls throughout the Somme and Marne valleys. Every town has a memorial marking the names of local soldiers and civilians who died "Pour la Gloire de La France". The photographs at Arras put faces to some of those who might be lying in in those very graveyards.

It was a bit incongruous to walk through the plaza and read the accounts of the struggle, while all around these pictures the Friday night crowd was enjoying a cool spring evening, laughing and talking as on any other weekend night. I had to stop and think about the ways we present art, the spaces we build to exhibit visual art, and the reasons why a city might decide to show these 100 photos in a location generally used for recreation and dining rather than contemplation of such a significant event.

For me, the concert hall, the museum, a theatre...these are sacred spaces, no less so than any religious structure claiming that description. It is in these places that we show who we really are, who we've been, who we hope to become. Where the arts live is the home of the creative soul of men and women. It is in these spaces that we show the deepest thoughts and feelings that men experience, the creative visions of women brought to reality in a way that bypasses our surface and reaches us at a different level.

As I walked through that exhibit, I was hypnotized by the power of the photographs. I wanted to stop, to get a drink and join the Friday night crowd. The power of the pictures was such that I couldn't stop, however, and so I continued round the plaza. After every stop, though, I was distracted by moving around another cafe table, or a server delivering hot hamburgers or crepes.

I began to see the placement of the pictures as perhaps an artistic statement in itself, but I have no way of knowing if this was intended. I'd like to have been at the meeting for the discussion that began with, "So...where should we show them?"

Saturday, 4/25/15--Rest day in Arras

Sunday, 4/26/15-- Arras to Bruay La Buissierres

This seemed like the first "suburban" day of the whole walk. I was on tiny country lanes and village streets for most of the day, walking through relatively new housing developments. Of course, every now and then, mixed in with the new homes is a century-old house, or a 200-

year old church, a 500-year-old barn. Much of this area was destroyed during wars from the last century, so there are lots of replacement buildings.

I was happy to have the sun again for awhile, but the rain caught me for the last two hours of the day. It wasn't heavy enough to really soak me, but it's just more tiring to walk in the wet.

Fortunately, I checked my phone messages and found voicemail from the hotel I'd tried to book. As do lots of family-run hotels here, they shut down for an afternoon or one day each week. Some don't take any guests for that day, but this one did. The owner gave me a code to a digital lock on the back door and told me he'd leave a key to my room inside the door. The staff went home at 2:00 Sunday afternoon and left the guests to take care of themselves. The system works, and I was happy to have a key to a warm dry room waiting.

Bruay is a good sized city, so I thought it would easy to find dinner. Not so. The town is spread out over several kilometers, and I had to walk two of them to find an open pizzeria. After a 29k day, I wasn't in the mood for that. Oddly enough, I had to walk the same two afterwards to get back to the hotel. Funny how that works.

Monday, 4/27/15--Bruay to Aire-sur-la-Lys

The weather turned on me again today--42F and windy. My old body can't decide whether it's time to shiver or sweat, so I did some of both today. The norther and the rain freshened the air, though, and the day was sparkling clear.

I had found another little hotel in the center of Aire-sur-la-Lys, but this owner told me that he shuts down every afternoon for siesta. He'd warned me not to show up till 4:30 as that's when he reopened for the evening. I took my time on the walk, stopping for a long lunch and an extra coffee in Lillers. Had another one at a McDonald's on the edge of Aire and took advantage of their free wifi to work a bit while I was waiting for Laurent to open his Hotel Europ for the afternoon.

Tuesday, 4/28/15--Aire to Wisques

Only two 23k days and an 18k, and I'll be at the coast. Hard to believe. When I look at my phone map now, I see a little edge of blue water on the left side. It makes me want to be aware of every step...which isn't hard since my feet are dead tired and sore and ready to stop walking.

I found an early bar open in Roquetoire and took advantage of a place to get out of the cool wind. I'd planned to work a little, but the bartender was bored and wanted to talk. The place looked recently re-done. When I asked if it was new, the owner told me it was only 200 years old. We talked a little history, a bit of travel, some war tales, skeet shooting ("ball trap" here), the weather, of course...everything but politics. I like a friendly bar.

Aside from a cool breeze, the spring weather made for nice walking. I even found a fine boulangerie open just 2k shy of Wisques and was able to pick up an afternoon treat.

I'd booked a nice hotel in the tiny village as it was the only lodging I could find at the halfway point between Aire and Ardres. (I was determined to make it to Ardres the next day so that I would have an easy 16k canal-walk as my last day into Calais.). I later discovered I could have requested pilgrim lodging in the giant old abbey in Wisques. They still brew beer there (Jenlain), and I think it would have been a fun experience. No matter, though...I was ready for a little luxury at the hotel. It was the only spot for dinner in town, and I took full advantage.

I was still full the next morning, but that didn't stop me from taking advantage of their big buffet breakfast. I wish I'd found the right size tray for the serving line, though...the one I had was small enough to tilt through the rails and spill hot coffee all over my crotch. (You can't take a country boy to the nice hotels, I guess.)

Wednesday, 4/29/15--Wisques to Ardres

I chose an easy, but slightly longer route today to get off of the busier roads. I knew what to expect in Ardres and didn't want to be cranky from fighting traffic when I got there. My track took me again through a chain of villages, over some rolling hills, and finally by a bar/cafe that was open. I'd already given up on a hot lunch and stopped for a pack snack at a gravel dump. (Any windbreak will do.) It was nice to pull into the bar for a hot drink, though. The place was crowded for lunch, but I found a high table with a stool off to one side. Leaned my pack against the wall--out of the way, I thought--and the next person through the door found a way to kick it over and knock over a metal trash can. All talking stopped, everyone looked my way. I just pointed silently at the guy that knocked it over and acted like it was his pack.

The rain hit again as I reached Ardres, but I had a nice room at a B&B owned by a retired British woman. I checked in and set up a Skype session with Cindy King, our International Languages Coordinator. After we worked our plan, I umbrella'd my way through the shower to the town center and a fun bar I'd spotted on my way through. Cindy and I set up a video chat with her beginning French class and gave them a tour of the town and cafe. The Owner of the Le Cosy Coza thought it was fun that we were doing a video class meeting in his bar. This is our cut-rate (but effective) style of international education.

Thursday, 4/30/15--Ardres to Calais!!!

My final 16k to the coast was a flat, beautiful path that began in the Ardres Thursday morning market and then through a straight path between the lakes north of the town. This is a popular recreation spot during the summer. Today I had it to myself along with a few strolling locals. I connected with the Canal de Halage that services Calais, but the day was so beautiful that I didn't want to hurry. I think I stopped every hour along the way for another coffee, trying to be aware that the long walk was nearing an end. After I reached Calais, I'd cross the Channel and have only two more half-day walks up to Canterbury. Reaching Calais felt in some respects like the end of the road.

When I finally reached the city, I found my hotel locked up. A sign on the door told me that reception was closed until 4pm. This had often been the case along the way. Since I was walking off-season for the hotels, I was finding there wasn't enough business for them to staff a front desk all day. I passed the time in yet another bar, and Cindy and I chatted with another of her classes. I'd like to have given them all a taste of the abbey-brewed beer I had, but that's beyond even Skype's capabilities. At the moment, anyway. Give it a few years, and there will be an app for that, I'm sure.

Friday, 5/1/15-- May Day

The town and I were celebrating. The sun came out -- occasionally, anyway--and fought a cool steady breeze on May Day. Calais put on a good face in spite of the wind chill. There were muguet tables set up two-to-a-block, stocked with buckets of lucky bouquets and staffed by either smiling little children or tired grandparents.

It felt great to have reached the coast, and I had taken a day off to relax, to stroll a little, maybe see a movie. It felt like a Saturday to me with the holiday in force.

I found a theatre where I'd seen a show the last time I was in town and laughed at the memory. That time I'd crossed on the ferry from the UK and forgotten the one-hour time change. I showed up at the ticket window, and the woman said she'd sell me a ticket, but that the picture was already forty-five minutes gone. I laughed and tried to explain what I'd done, and she just nodded politely like she was taking care of a senile uncle.

Well, this time I double-checked the time just to be sure. It wasn't the same woman at the ticket booth, but she had the same expression as she explained--in slow and careful French--that this was Friday, not Saturday, that the movie I wanted wouldn't be shown that day. I'm just snakebit there, I guess. I tried to go back later for a different movie, but they'd put my photo in the window with a circle around me and a line through my face.

I thought I'd feel a little more like celebrating when I arrived here, but the truth is that it's been a sobering last few weeks walking through all the WWI & WWII battlefields and cemeteries. Almost every town I passed has a marker or two honoring their "...enfants mort pour la gloire de France", and there's hardly an hour of walking that hasn't led me beside another walled orchard of white military crosses. Most mark French graves, but other thousands are for those from Commonwealth countries, the U.S., from Germany, graves of soldiers from every continent.

Most of the physical damage of the wars has of course been repaired or covered over, but some will never be "fixed". According to one memorial site maintained by Souvenir Francais, an association that maintains war memorials, 27 entire towns in Northern France were destroyed in WWII and never rebuilt. The numbers of dead and wounded are too staggering to comprehend, and I found myself thinking about them for hours as I walked.

I remembered the photographic exhibition in Arras at their Place des Heros in remembrance of the hundredth anniversary of WWI, some showing the smiling, happy, patriotic faces of the teenagers heading into the war, and others revealing the physical and emotional devastation of the years of conflict.

As I was trying to wrap my mind around those events, a current war intruded. The British host of a B&B in Ardres where I spent a night told me that she retired after years working for the company that operates the Chunnel between France and England. She warned me to be prepared for delays trying to cross the Channel because of crowds of immigrants at the ferry port. I started looking for a ferry ticket today and found all sorts of rough stories about crowds of Middle Eastern immigrants here trying to force their way onto trucks and boats to slip into the UK, where apparently it's easier to survive without papers. Local officials and relief groups have worked to calm that crisis and build relief camps nearby.

I walked on out to the ferry port this morning to see if it was going to be an issue, and it's not...I already have a ticket for tomorrow morning early. The immediacy of that crisis has passed, but there was a heavy armed police presence. Here also remains lots of graffiti on the way to the boat...the idea of "F**k Privilege" being the general theme. It feels bad to be on the privilege end of that sentiment, but I'm sure it's a lot worse on the other end. I thought again--a bit guiltily this time-- how lucky I am to be able to walk on into the port with my US passport and credit card and buy whatever I need, to leave at will.

I was following this story closer when I was in Italy, one of the main pipelines for the war refugees into Europe. The Mediterranean versions of coyotes are squeezing these unfortunates for everything they have, packing them onto junker boats, then disabling them off the coast of Italy. The Italians have no choice but to rescue these people--when they can reach them in time--but Italy's economy is itself in the dumpster. They have no resources to handle the crowds. Lots of new arrivals are walking/working their way up here to Calais as a possible way of entry to the UK. My Brit friend believes the influx is fueling UK's New Nationalist Party, their version of our Let's-Build-A-Wall-At-The-Border group. It's a sad, tough situation for everyone involved.

But, deservedly or not, I'm able to leave at will. Since I was able to land a ticket, I plan to hit the ferry early Saturday morning, land in Dover mid-morning, and do the final two short days of walking up to the cathedral at Canterbury. My boots are about gone, but strategic application of a roll of the Arkansas Bandaid (duct tape), should hold them together for two more days. I'll leave them in a rubbish bin at the cathedral.

[Note: Within three months of the writing of this passage, the violence in Syria had worsened and a fresh flood of refugees fleeing that devastation was pouring onto the continent. At this writing, the "jungle", the makeshift refugee camp in Calais is being bulldozed and the temporary residents relocated. At the same time, however, two local organizations are building more comfortable semi-permanent structures for the same refugees, trying to offer them better living conditions.]

Saturday, 5/2/15—

Was up and out early for the ferry, and it was a good thing. I remembered being grilled pretty hard at British Passport Control the last time I crossed the border on foot and had allowed extra time for that. It was a good thing I did. Though there were only a dozen foot passengers lined up for security check, the interview that normally takes 30 seconds took me 15 minutes. The guard was calm and nice about it, but he wanted to make sure I wasn't going to be a drain on the UK economy. I had to show him a passport, driver's license, debit card, credit cards, proof of health insurance, my pilgrim's credential, my British Library card, a picture of my boat, the name of my first elementary school, my second nephew's favorite color...by the end of the chat I think we'd actually signed a pre-nuptial. Not sure...but he's promised to call.

I landed in Dover to light rain and hiked on out to Shepherds Well, half way to Canterbury. Took the train back into town to a sweet B&B with a hyper-attentive couple. They met me at the door with smiles, a cup of tea, and more info about Dover cafes than anyone could eat.

It felt a bit surreal that night, knowing the next morning would end the walk. Rain was in the forecast, and I thought of waiting for a sunny Monday. I couldn't wait to be done, though.

Sunday, 5/3/15—

After a great made-to-order breakfast, I loaded the pack for a rainy hike for the last time. I got an early train out to Shepherds Well and headed for my final target. The rain soaked me for an hour or two, the wind blew me about between the hedgerows for another hour, but then the sun finally popped out as I passed the golf club and reached the edge of Canterbury.

I hiked straight on into the cathedral grounds to the window of their welcome booth to get a stamp on my credential...and they were closed. Slipped into the cathedral even though they were closed to visitors, but I found no one there either who had a stamp.

Finally gave up and just stopped at the cathedral book store. I could have hung around for services and found a cleric to help me, but by then I was done, ready to kick off the boots and quit.

I asked a little old guy with a camera to take my picture at the cathedral so I'd have proof that I made it. He got down on his knees, intent on getting the whole tower in the photo. Then he lay down on his side...his wife was rolling her eyes. Mr. Photog...he was so focused on the tower, he almost missed me. Whatever...I made it, and the boots were the next morning on the street by the trash can. (Later in the afternoon they we're gone, but I don't know if they walked away on someone's feet or are feeding a Brit landfill.)

WALKING THROUGH AN ENCYCLOPEDIA

As I relive this walk through words on pages, my mind spins through a dozen years of walking these two trails--EL CAMINO DE SANTIAGO and LA VIA FRANCIGENA. I'm struck by the history and culture(s) condensed into these two roads, the wealth of wisdom, knowledge, art, music, history encountered during the walks.

The idea that keeps coming back to me is that following these two trails is a walk through an encyclopedia, bumping every day into another author, painter, setting for an opera, tale of a warrior or peacemaker, another sinner or saint.

The last 500 miles of the Spanish camino begins in a picturesque French village, but the first day's trail leads high over the Pyrennees, not far from where Hannibal's war elephants traveled toward Rome in 218 a.d.

Before that first day's hike is finished, pilgrims pass the point where Roland blew his horn. He and his few men were the rear guard for Charlemagne's army, and their last and fatal stand in 718 inspired the Song of Roland, the oldest surviving epic poem in French literature.

The route continues through Basque villages and farms, crossing streams that Hemingway mentions in his writings. This is one area he loved to visit for the fishing.

Hemingway is always connected in the minds of Americans with the running of the Bulls in Pamplona.

Often pilgrims passing through that walled city will plan an extra stop to experience that cultural phenomena.

The Camino winds through the Basque territory for the first week of the walk. One early stop in a Basque bar for a cafe' con leche led me into a conversation with the owner, a friendly sort who wanted to show off his command of English.

He told me how, long ago, some American men from Idaho and the Dakotas had ventured here and returned home with Basque women as wives. Basque men had responded by traveling that far and finding their own choices among some Native American tribes, eventually arriving back home with a significant number of Shoshone women. "In fact", he told me, "we still use the slang 'shosho' to refer to someone who doesn't know our local customs that well."

I confessed that I didn't know much about the Basque region, that most of what I knew had come from reports of bombs set by Basque separatists. The mood suddenly changed, and he fixed me with a stare. "But if we don't do that," he declared, "the world will never hear of our situation."

I paid the tab and headed on down the trail, deciding that, if he didn't actually light the fuse, he was probably at the committee meeting that planned it.

The trail is rich with the history of Spain and the Catholic traditions of Western Europe. The cathedral at Burgos is one of the most beautiful gothic structures on the continent, and countless smaller chapels and churches offer surprising beauty in almost every village.

The Knights Templar were assigned to guard pilgrims on the Camino as part of their religious duties. The route is populated with bits and pieces of that history, including a grand, restored fortress above the river in Ponferrada. At the albergue in Manjarin, the highest in elevation along the French Route, the hospitalero considers himself an active member of the lost fraternity of holy knights. He and his helpers can often be seen wearing white tunics bearing the red crusader's cross.

As peregrinos climb the mountain to Galicia, the wind carries the sounds of bagpipes and pennywhistles as the flavor of the music from that region reflects their Celtic roots. Castilian Spanish gives way to the Gallegos hat welcomes walkers to the fabled city of Santiago de Compostela.

Reading these bits of history can be fascinating, but walking through them breathes life into printed facts.

Likewise, the Via Francigena is an illuminated manuscript of its own. For my walk this year the ancient Roman pavers on the Appia Antica began the trail through tombs, sculptures, catacombs, chapels.

A visit to Vatican City for a stamp of approval on my pilgrim's passport led me beside Michelangelo's Pieta, beside Bernini's Baldachin over Peter's tomb, and back out through the heart of the basilica. I exited to stand in early morning sun before St. Peter's Square, feeling as if I'd been given a license to be there.

Viterbo is a city-stop on the route with beautiful sections of the medieval wall still intact. A wonderful story of official inefficiency is told there--the tale of how in 1268-71 the cardinals supposed to be choosing a new pope were unable to agree...for three years. Local magistrates, weary of the ridiculous infighting, removed the roof and reduced the cardinals' rations to bread and water to hurry along the process

The heart of Tuscany provides decoration for a piece of the trail. Rolling green hills and rows of sentinel trees grace the route.

Lucca, another city with defensive walls still standing, claims the composer Puccini as one of its own. His music can be heard every day of the year on the streets and in concerts throughout the city.

Passing the lake where Puccini kept a home near Viareggio, pilgrims reach the coast and taste the breezes from the Ligurian Sea. Viareggio is at the foot of the marble mountains at Carrara. It is from these mountains near Massa and Carrara that Leonardo and others found the marble for their creations.

Walking through Pietrasanta, the location of Michelangelo's quarry, it is easy to imagine that the seniors sipping vino rosso at the cafes there today may have had relatives sitting nearby with their own glasses back during the Renaissance years, offering their opinions of the artist, his work, and the government of their day.

I stepped off the trail there, walked beside the sea, and found mounds of marble pebbles washed down from the quarries to the shore, worn smooth by the waves and wind. I had to wonder if one of those very pieces of marble may have flown from Michelangelo's chisel as he freed his David from a Pietrasanta column of white stone.

It was beside this sea where one dark afternoon Percy Bysshe Shelley met the storm that would claim his life. It was just a few miles east of the trail, along the beach at Lerici, where some days after the accident his body washed ashore and his friends built his funeral pyre.

The encyclopedic journey continues inland to Pontremoli, where stele and menhirs 5000 years old have been found. The trail rises, climbs over the Cisa Pass and across the Taro, passing near Bussetto, the birthplace of Giuseppe Verdi.

A week farther to the north hikers pass through the shadow of the Forti de Bard, where a small garrison of men delayed Napoleon's mighty army on its march to Rome. Today that picturesque redoubt is a museum and favorite movie set when Hollywood wants the look of an impregnable fortress.

Continuing on the trail leads pilgrims up through the Aosta Valley and toward the St. Bernard Pass. For centuries the Brothers there at the border with Switzerland have maintained a home for pilgrims, tired from their trek up the Alps. Members of that order also bred the famous Alpine rescue dogs that still bear the name of their patron saint.

The Swiss leg leads down into a fertile valley at Martigny and beside a Roman Coloseum. The lake at the mouth of that valley connects Montreux to Geneva and has generated its own inspiration for Stravinsky, Hindemith...and Freddie Mercury. Byron and the Shelleys lived for a time on its shores, and Frankenstein was born there.

Just north of the Jura Mountains pilgrims find the source of the Loue River and enter Ornans, birthplace of Renoir.

Napoleon's history intersects the route once again here near Bar sur Aube, where he rested his army for a long two weeks, deciding whether to attack a cavalry there or hurry to Paris to defend the city. While he waited, the city fell, and the general retired, soon to be forced into exile.

Other military ghosts populate the trail ahead in the Marne and Somme Valleys, notable as bearing witness to some of the most devastating scenes of battle in both World Wars. The cemeteries and monuments recreate pictures of incredible hardship, heroism, and the waste of human life on an unbelievable scale.

The trail finds the English Channel at Wisques near Calais, where stands a powerful bronze by Rodin, depicting the anguish and determination of a handful of town leaders willing to sacrifice themselves to save their friends.

It was at Calais in this summer of 2015 that my pilgrimage bumped into the current news as that city is one target of thousands of Syrian and North African refugees who were fleeing wars in their own countries to struggle toward the possibility of a better life in the UK.

Just across that stretch of water, barely visible on clear mornings, are the white cliffs of Dover, the "trailhead" to Canterbury, fabled by Chaucer in his Canterbury Tales and in T.S. Eliot's play, Murder in the Cathedral.

This outline of highlights is only a hint of the wealth of stories and images, sights and soundtracks of the Via Francigena and El Camino de Santiago. The list is long, though, and the memories vivid enough to make me forget the pain that comes with walking over a thousand miles. I'm ready to load the pack and start again today.

DENOUEMENT
LESSONS FROM THE TRAILS

Self-imposed limits. They're on my mind today as I start to try and wrap up this book. We build walls around our lives, often without even noticing that we're doing so. We brick up the openings so that no light peeks in, and we can't peek out. We can't see the glimmer of possibilities, the light of what could be. We squint so hard that we can't bring into focus those horizons that are actually not that far away.

I'm looking back on five months of walking and remembering the first few times I went on "long" walks. One wasn't a walk, but a slow run. It was a long-ago high school afternoon when a coach punished a few of us who had missed a workout by making us run extra laps. It was at the end of practice, and he had us jog an extra mile to remind us of our screwup. At the end of the mile, It hit me that I wasn't really very tired, and that at my slow pace, I could run farther. I kept making laps on that old dirt track around the football field for another hour or so, interested to observe that once you start rolling at an even pace, inertia can carry you forward for a long time.

Remember that this was back in the Dark Ages, back before the running-for-health craze hit America and marathons sprouted like weeds. Running shoes hadn't really been invented yet, and we ran barefoot or in cheap little track flats.

A few years later, but still back in my youth (I was 30?), I'd had a car break down on the way home from work. I left it in a shop next to where it stopped. I caught a ride home, but when it was time to pick it up, no one was available. I decided to walk to the shop to get the car, to walk the entire--gasp--six miles.

I'm not sure why this particular incident seems like such a breakwater event. I'd been an off-and-on jogger for years by then and had run lots of 5k-10ks. I have a clear memory, though, that this was somehow different, that the walking somehow made this an awakening of sorts. The idea was planted then, I think, that I could walk long distances, and that for some reason this was a revelation.

Later years saw day hikes with friends and hiking clubs, but I never even really considered a longer distance--a life-changing distance--until decades later I was drawn suddenly to try El Camino in Spain one summer. There was no real planning or preparation...I just decided one day to do it, and the next day I was on a plane to Spain.

The impact of that first pilgrimage was immediate and profound. It moved me in unexpected ways, and it was clear to me as I was reaching my goal that I wanted more. I've become addicted to the walking, and as soon as the pain of one walk fades, I find myself looking for another trail or a chance to revisit a familiar one. I think I'm still learning from the walks, but I keep coming back for more.

I'm a slow student, but a persistent one. Every walk is a self-contained little world with its own context, history, its own population of pilgrims and observers, supporters and critics. Some of the lessons learned along the way are painful, some are silly, some make me dope slap myself and say, " Why didn't I know that already?"

A few things I've noticed from the last few thousand miles of walking:

1) It hurts. It occasionally hurts a lot. And, it hurts so good. I think there's maybe a clear connection between the level of discomfort and the impact on your life. Does it date me to say that I still believe in the old adage of No Gain without the Pain? I know there was a movement back in the eighties (or was it the nineties?) to kill that idea, back around the time where it became a practice to call everyone a winner, to hand out participation ribbons to everyone who showed up. I'm a believer in showing up, too, and in encouraging beginnings, but I also believe we need to teach the value of working through the pain to reach a euphoric reward.

2) There's no better way to see a country than on your feet, at a walking pace. In the US, our lives are planned around automobiles. Unless you live in one of the few cities with major public transport systems, Americans drive. Everywhere. We drive to work, to play...we drive to the gym to go get some exercise. We may pay for that expensive gym membership, but we'll also circle the parking lot at the big box stores looking for a parking place closest to the front door.

Walking through a country slows you down from driving speed to a pace where you can actually smell and taste the country. Things too small to notice through the window of a moving car are suddenly elevated in size and importance.

Our lives fly past us, and moving at speed means that the landscape around us flies past as well. Slow down to a walk, and your perspective on life changes to match that speed. Your vision will become more acute as you begin to notice what you've missed through the shield of a car window.

3) Everyone has a story. If you take the time to listen, you'll hear amazing tales along the way. Another benefit of the pilgrim's pace is that it removes distractions, giving walkers time to talk and to listen.

4) The pilgrimages draw a different collection of people and stories. Everyone does have a story, true, but the ones who are drawn to travel from half a world away to walk for a month or two or six often have particularly captivating tales to tell of what led them to the walking life.

5) Old World history is a deep, rich one, filled with drama, love, art, literature, tragedy, and triumph. Walking the pilgrimage trails is a vital way to live that history.

6) Lightening your load is the best way to lose weight--the superfluous pounds of stuff and worry we've all become used to carrying everywhere we go. Live out of a backpack for a month, and you'll find how freeing it is to live with less.

7) Walking across a country will open you to believing that more dreams are within your reach...and you'll be right.

Buen Camino!